Laura Ream

History of a Trip to the Great Saginaw Valley, June, 1871

By invitation of the Fort Wayne, Muncie, and Cincinnati railroad

Laura Ream

History of a Trip to the Great Saginaw Valley, June, 1871
By invitation of the Fort Wayne, Muncie, and Cincinnati railroad

ISBN/EAN: 9783337197209

Printed in Europe, USA, Canada, Australia, Japan

Cover: Foto ©Andreas Hilbeck / pixelio.de

More available books at **www.hansebooks.com**

HISTORY OF A TRIP

TO THE

GREAT SAGINAW VALLEY,

JUNE, 1871.

BY INVITATION OF

THE FORT WAYNE, MUNCIE, AND CINCINNATI RAILROAD,

AND WITH THE CO-OPERATION OF THE

BEE LINE, FORT WAYNE, JACKSON AND SAGINAW, AND JACKSON, LANSING AND SAGINAW RAILROAD COMPANIES.

BY LAURA REAM.

INDIANAPOLIS:
R. J. BRIGHT & CO., PRINTERS.
1871.

PREFACE.

"You have been elected historian of our excursion." This is what Mr. Keating said to me on our return trip. With visions of kind faces, beautiful places, saw mills, saw-dust and salt floating through my mind, it was a full second before I comprehended his meaning. Then I was surprised and gratified. Considering myself a party by favor in that delightful excursion, it was an unexpected honor, of a piece with the uniform kindness shown me by the press. To express, in some sense, my obligations, I can only repeat what, from the fullness of my heart, I said to him:

"I am afraid I can not do justice to the subject, but I am grateful for the commission, and you may be sure I will do the best I can."

Just here, I desire to thank the members of the press for copies of their valuable reports of the excursion. In view of these charming and complete reports, I have scarcely had courage to perform my task. Any one of them is so much better than I can write, that I have been constantly tempted to make a souvenir job of it by compiling something from each rich tribute to the liberality and enterprise of the Fort Wayne, Muncie and Cincinnati Editorial Excursion to Saginaw Bay—but this would not, strictly speaking, be a history—and, in the weakness of my endeavor, I must crave the further indulgence of my fellow-excursionists and friends.

LAURA REAM.

INDIANAPOLIS, July 15, 1871.

CONTENTS.

6

CHAPTER XII.

CHAPTER XIII.

CHAPTER XIV.

CHAPTER XV.

TESTIMONIALS.

A TRIP

TO THE

GREAT SAGINAW VALLEY.

CHAPTER I.

OUR INVITATION.

Our invitation was printed in bronze, with an ornamental border, on handsome note paper, and read:

FORT WAYNE, MUNCIE & CINCINNATI R. R.,
MUNCIE ROUTE,
FORT WAYNE, IND., MAY 22, 1871.

Dear Sir: Yourself and Lady are respectfully invited to participate in an Editorial Excursion to Saginaw Bay, on Tuesday, June 6, 1871.

PROGRAMME.

The Excursion Train will start from Connersville, Ind., June 6th, at 10 A. M., via this Road, and a Special Car will leave Indianapolis, via "Bee Line," at 10:55 A. M., June 6th, arriving in Fort Wayne at 4:35 P. M.

After a night's rest, the party will take Special Train on the Fort Wayne, Jackson and Saginaw R. R., to Jackson, Mich., and thence via Jackson, Lansing and Saginaw R. R. to Saginaw Bay, arriving there the evening of the 7th.

W. W. WORTHINGTON, *Sup't.*

JNO. J. GRAFTON, *Gen'l Ticket Agt.*

2

By arrangement· these Invitations will be honored for passage, going and returning, by the Roads above named. You will confer a favor by informing the undersigned at your earliest convenience whether you can be with us, in order that every arrangement may be made for the comfort of the party.

JNO. J. GRAFTON,
General Ticket Agent, Fort Wayne.

Upon receipt of which we, each and severally, had recourse to a map in order to ascertain just where we were expected. In this I do not write from personal experience alone, for I was assured, on the excursion, that not one of the party had ever been to Saginaw Bay before, or had had the least idea of its precise location.

Since my return, I have found the public, generally, possessed of but a vague impression, and for the enlightenment of such, as also for the convenience of those unable to participate in the excursion, I have been at great pains to secure and prefix A MAP OF THE GREAT SAGINAW ROUTE, for which I am indebted to our prince of hosts, John J. Grafton.

That most enterprising of journalists, Mr. Shurich, suggested that a map of our route would enhance the value of my work. Whereupon, I consulted charts and chart-makers with very little chance of having the idea carried out. In my extremity I wrote to Mr. Grafton, who, in the absence of a map, supplied me with one of his own design. He was very modest about it, but it struck me as admirable, and I carried it at once to the best lithographer in Indianapolis, who pronounced it "splendid," and "worth the price of the book." I do not need to say any more; it carries recommendation on its face.

The reader will see at a glance that Saginaw Bay runs out like a thumb half way down the Michigan coast of Lake Huron, and that to get there by the Fort Wayne, Muncie and Cincinnati, the Fort Wayne, Jackson and Saginaw, and the Jackson, Lansing and Saginaw Railroads, is to pursue a bee-line north a little further from Chicago than Toledo. The innumerable railway connections will be observed, especially the projected line to Mackinaw, Duluth, Puget's Sound and China. Running the eye downward on the map, the principal resting points are Indianapolis, Cincinnati and Louisville; the nether points of Nashville, Memphis, Mobile, New Orleans and Texas placed in bold relief.

The question, What of it? naturally arising, I answer, Behold!

THE SHORT CUT TO THE REGIONS OF LUMBER AND SALT.

In other words, this route may be likened to a great chute whereby the rich treasures of the North are precipitated into the lap of the South and South West. The figure is not strained, when we consider, how far the speedy transportation of these staples will go toward the commercial and visible reconstruction of the South. In return, for it is a chute which works both ways, the South will find a ready market for its valuable products. But this is anticipating what was better said on our memorable trip.

CHAPTER II.

THE COMPANY WE HAD.

The main portion of invited guests, under charge of Mr. W. W. Worthington, Superintendent of the Fort Wayne, Muncie and Cincinnati Railroad, were joined at Muncie by a number from Indianapolis, Terre Haute, Louisville and Memphis, in care of Mr. John J. Grafton, General Ticket Agent of the above-mentioned road. Mr. Grafton was accompanied by his wife, a lovely young lady. It was yet too soon, and the opportunity was not favorable, to know the company we had, but we were, at once, made sensible of our good fortune in falling into the hands of the officers of that road. Superintendent Worthington had an eye single to the comfort of his guests, and Mr. Grafton was fairly ubiquitous in the art of pleasing.

The weather, that 6th of June, was intensely hot, and as we struck out of the clearings at Muncie there did not seem to be a breath of air. The sun shone like a ball of fire in a sky at white heat; when, suddenly, without the warning of a cloud or peal of thunder, the heavens were overspread with darkness and there fell a drenching rain. It dashed on the roof, against the windows and upon the sides of the cars, the welcome, bountiful and refreshing rain ! We enjoyed it as much as the hungry and athirst, parched earth.

I could not understand why the cloud seemed to have settled on the brow of Mr. Worthington, and Mr. Grafton had a look of care in his face not unlike that of a housewife whose "cake's all dough." At length the cars stopped at a beautiful grove, where we beheld

A FRUSTRATED PICNIC.

Do I need to paint the picture? The dripping rain, the dripping townsfolk and country people, the dripping band of music, the soggy pine tables and worse than soggy victuals. The only water proof substance was a hamper of wine, and, by odd chance, that was the first to be rescued from the rain. Now it transpired that the good Railroad Company, Ft. W., M. and C., had arranged this picnic at Keystone for the happiness of their guests and to promote general acquaintance. The much needed, generous rain had come half a day too soon. Hence the anxious faces I have described. The Company did the next best thing they could. They took the people, musicians and provender aboard, and while the dripping waiters served the soggy victuals and water proof libations, the Hon. F. P. Randall, Mayor of Fort Wayne, tendered us the hospitalities of that city. Here, be it said, that his Honor, in his genial countenance, rounded figure and eloquent grace, would serve for the personification of welcome. His address was replete with the spirit of fraternity and enterprise, and was an earnest of the courtesies extended us in Fort Wayne. Before describing *them*, it will be proper to give a list of our party as assigned to the hospitalities of that city :

OUR PARTY.

Rev. A. CONVERSE and Wife, *Christian Observer*, Louisville, Ky.

J. H. TURNER, Esq., Wife and Child, *Industrial and Commercial Gazette*, Louisville, Ky.

Mr. E. WHITMORE and Wife, *Public Ledger*, Memphis, Tenn.

Mr. J. M. KEATING and Wife, *Appeal*, Memphis, Tenn.

Mr. P. S. WESTFALL and Wife, *Express*, Terre Haute, Ind.

Mrs. MILLIGAN, Terre Haute, Ind.

Mr. HOWARD BRIGGS and Wife, *The Press*, Greencastle, Ind.

Mr. S. MERRILL and Wife, *Muncie Telegraph*, Indianapolis.

Mr. A. J. HALFORD, *Journal*, Indianapolis.

Mr. W. B. VICKERS, *Saturday Evening Mirror*, Indianapolis.

Mr. B. D. JONES and Wife, *Commercial*, Indianapolis.

Mr. A. M. BENHAM, Wife and Child, *Musical Review*, Indianapolis.

Mr. CHARLES P. JACOBS, Wife, Child and Servant, *News*, Indianapolis.

LAURA REAM, *Cincinnati Commercial*, Indianapolis.

LIVINGSTON DUNLAP, Indianapolis.

Mr. J. O. HARDESTY and Wife, *Herald*, Anderson, Ind.

Mr. CHARLES H. NIX and Wife, Huntington, Ind.

Mr. JOHN MARSH and Wife, Muncie, Ind.

GAZZAM GANO, J. L. HAVEN, MILES GREENWOOD, Committee from Board of Trade, Cincinnati, Ohio.

T. R. BIGGS, L. H. SARGENT, H. L. LAWS, Committee from Chamber of Commerce, Cincinnati, Ohio.

Mr. A. L. ANDREWS, *Merchants' and Manufacturers' Bulletin*, Cincinnati, Ohio.

CINCINNATI DELEGATES AT LARGE.

Mr. and Mrs. LEWIS WORTHINGTON, L. S. WORTHINGTON, M. D., Mr. JOSEPH KINSEY, Mr. OLIVER KINSEY, Mrs. MILES GREENWOOD, Mrs. T. R. BIGGS, Mrs. J. H. LAWS, Mrs. G. GANO, two Children and Servant, Miss SALLIE MEAD, Miss MAGGIE BONNER, Miss HATTIE GANO, Prof. C. G. COMEGYS.

Mr. A. C. MELLETT and Wife, *Times*, Muncie, Ind.

Mr. E. R. ZELLER, *Citizen*, Oxford, Ohio.

Miss SUE E. TIMBERMAN, Oxford, Ohio.

Mr. C. F. JACKSON, *Democrat*, Hartford City, Ind.

BRUCE MOFFATT and Wife, *Republican*, Springfield, Ohio.

Mr. JOHN A. BEVERIDGE and Wife, *Gazette*, Xenia, Ohio.

Mr. W. J. CRAIG, *Banner*, Bluffton, Ind.

Mr. JOHN M. HIGGS and Wife, *Examiner*, Connersville, Ind.

Mr. SAMUEL SHAFFER, *Democrat*, Muncie, Ind.

Mr. A. G. WILCOX, *Courier*, Newcastle, Ind.

Mr. M. L. BUNDY, Newcastle, Ind.

Miss BUNDY, Newcastle, Ind.

Mr. E. H. BUNDY and Wife, *Times*, Newcastle, Ind.

Mr. GEORGE S. BROWN, Huntington, *Indiana Herald*, Bluffton, Ind.

The roll of passengers thus called, it is high time to pay our respects to the bridge that carried us over

THE FORT WAYNE, MUNCIE AND CINCINNATI RAILROAD.

This road was first built from Connersville to Newcastle several years ago, (the exact date I have not been able to learn) and operated by the Cincinnati & Indianapolis Junction Railroad Company, who completed and ran it to Muncie, in 1869. The road was then extended to Fort Wayne, and completed in September, 1870, though not in good condition for business. In January, 1871, a company known as the "Muncie Transportation Company," backed by the distinguished capitalists, John Jacob Astor, and Moses Taylor, of New York, Baring brothers, of New York, and London, and John W. Forbes, of Boston, purchased the line from Connersville to Fort Wayne, a distance of 109 miles, and immediately went to work with a large force of men to put the entire line in the very best working order. They stocked the road with new engines and cars of every kind, and expect, by the coming fall, to have it in prime condition.

The road is built in almost a straight line, and runs through a new but magnificent country. The wealth of the agricultural districts is fast pouring in on the line, and towns, villages, and manufactures are springing into importance. It is too soon to count large dividends, but it may be confidently asserted that the road is now established upon a sure and paying basis.

THE OFFICERS OF THE FT. W., M. & C. R. R.

C. H. DALTON, President, Boston, Mass.

W. W. WORTHINGTON, General Superintendent, Fort Wayne, Ind.

C. S. WOODWARD, Chief Engineer, Fort Wayne, Ind.

JNO. J. GRAFTON, General Ticket Agent, Fort Wayne, Ind.

J. C. BRINSLEY, Master Transportation, Fort Wayne, Ind.

R. GLYNN, Master Mechanic, Fort Wayne, Ind.

A. H. STEWART, Superintendent of Bridges, Fort Wayne, Ind.

D. R. BONNELL, Superintendent of Telegraph, Fort Wayne, Ind.

On the brilliant occasion, when in the words of a fellow-excursionist, " Jno. J. Grafton took a ride, and we were there to see." Mr. P. H. Ashley was conductor, and John McCullom, Engineer.

CHAPTER III.

FORT WAYNE.

The citizens of Fort Wayne met us at the depot in carriages, many of them of the most elegant description, and conducted us over the city. By this time the rain had subsided to a misty drizzle, notwithstanding which, the streets were crowded with men, women, and children, in holiday attire. The first object of interest, after the gay spectacle of people, was the Catholic possessions, being a square or block right in the heart of the city, occupied by the Cathedral, Bishop's Palace, College and Convent. Two of our party, Mrs. Worthington, and Miss Bonner, of Cincinnati, had the pleasure of a visit with their old friend, the Right Rev. Lauers, Bishop of Fort Wayne, and in view of his sudden death, it must be a sacred souvenir to them.

The Court House is an attractive point, occupying as it does an entire block, surrounded by ornamental grounds and fence, and the center of four handsomely built blocks, with flag stone side walks, and Nicholson pavements.

In our drive we passed through several handsomely built business streets, and saw any number of beautiful dwelling houses. Many of them were really elegant. Thence to the Pittsburgh, Fort Wayne, and Chicago railroad shops, the largest in the city. They are built of brick in the most substantial manner, and form quite a town of themselves, giving employment to 1,500 men, and paying out $300,000 a month for material and labor. Then, in order, comes the Toledo, Wabash and Western shops, which employ 400 men. The great car wheel factory of Mr. J. H. Bass, gives employment to 300 men, and expends at least $120,000 per month for material and labor.

A leading work of interest is the carriage wood work and buggy wheel manufactory of Olds & Son, giving employment to 250 men, the product of whose labor finds a market in Europe, and North and South America.

A notable object of interest was Hoffman's patent Band Saw Mill, which is destined to work a revolution in the machinery of saw mills.

The standing room of the mill does not occupy a space of more than twenty by forty feet, including the groove upon which the log to be sawed is projected from and against the saw. The engine, some ten feet in length and six in hight, is to the right of the shed. The saw, forty feet in length, four or five inches wide, and joined at the ends, revolves continuously in an elliptical line around a nether and upper pulley, six feet apart. These pulleys are six feet in diameter, and the lower one, hidden from view by the floor of the mill, is the driving one, while the upper one is on the strain, or keeps the saw in place. The motion of the saw is regulated by the box of cone shaped grooves, acting one upon another, subject to the lever, tension, or break of the mechanical paradox, commonly called "feed," for which the inventor, Mr. Hoffman, has a separate patent. The log in position on the trucks, it is passed backward and forward on the minature railroad, the saw cutting it in the desired manner.

Mr. Hoffman spent fifteen years of labor and anxious thought upon his invention before he succeeded in perfecting it. The patent was obtained June 6, 1869. It is constructed on the principle of the little circular saws which have been in use for several years. It is the first application to the sawing of logs. Its advantages over the ordinary circular saw are:

First—In the saving of lumber, cutting one-twelfth of an inch saw-herf, while an ordinary saw cuts five-sixteenths; there is a saving of two hundred and twenty-nine feet in each one thousand feet of timber, which, in valuable timber, would save the cost of machine in six months.

Second—Saving of power. Ten-horse power is all that is required to cut five or six thousand feet of hard or soft timber a day.

Third—Making better timber, leaving no offset.

Lastly—The entire safety of the saw.

The saw blade is manufactured in Paris.

To give an idea of the unexampled prosperity of Fort Wayne, I have only to state, that in 1860 the population was less than 11,000, now it is differently estimated at from 26,000 to 30,000. It has an air of great commercial wealth, and uncommon sumptuousness of living. I may add that if live newspapers and splendid school buildings are any indication of metropolitan standing, Fort Wayne may take rank with the most flourishing cities in the country.

"Where is French Town?" I asked of my host who had called my attention to the citizens of French descent, who were seen on every hand.

"There is scarcely any of the old town left," he replied.

I found upon inquiry, that the early French settlers had

rapidly affiliated with the English, and had thus, in the course of a couple of generations, lost their distinctive nationality, in this respect, varying from the French of Vincennes.

I had the pleasure of sojourning in one of the oldest places in Fort Wayne.

THE FORMER HOME OF THE HON. HUGH M'CULLOUGH.

It is now occupied by his son, Mr. Charles McCullough, and his family. It is an old fashioned frame dwelling, two stories in height, with wide portico in front, supported by heavy columns reaching to the main roof. There is a wide hall in the center of the building running past double parlors on one side, and library and family room on the other, terminating in the dining room. The second floor is well arranged, and like every other part of the house, handsomely furnished, the pictures and books being of rare value. In front are charming old grounds, with a rose plat and fountain at the foot of the steps. In every direction are majestic trees, planted, many of them, by the mother of Mr. McCullough. To the left, the grounds slope abruptly to the St. Mary's river, the ripple of whose waters falls like music on the ear. There is many a charming nook on the bank, which, but over the way from the busy town, is yet as retired as a dell. What trees to read a book in, and it made my heart ache to be a child again; just to swing out, by my hands, on a limb over the stream.

No wonder the old servitor called it "a purty place," and thought "Misther McCullough must often been a thinking of it in his new home in Lunnen."

THE BANQUET AT THE RINK.

As if private hospitality was not enough, the good citizens of Fort Wayne, in the Rink assembled, gave the excursionists a public reception. It was an uncommonly brilliant assemblage. The display of fine toilets was not surpassed by the superb display of flowers, and there was nothing wanting to make the banquet a success: delicious refreshments—it was all refreshment, after our days ride—the gay scene, the ravishing music, delicious viands, sparkling wine, and flow of soul. Mayor Randall presided. On taking the chair, he repeated the welcome so graciously extended on the cars, and in this connection expressed his obligations to Mr. Worthington, of Cincinnati, for having built the Muncie railroad. To his enterprise was the North mainly indebted for the opportunity of exchanging courtesies with their Southern neighbors. His Honor then made an interesting summary of the commercial wealth of Fort Wayne, citing the manufacture of $600,000 worth of car wheels for one example. He remarked, that twenty-five years ago, the trade of Fort Wayne was almost exclusively with Cincinnati, but latterly had been diverted into other channels, and that the object of this excursion was to show the great facilities of the new route from the Ohio river to the Lakes.

Mr. Joseph Kinsey, of the Cincinnati Board of Trade, replied. His first words were that he hoped that the large and profitable trade that had once existed between Cincinnati and Fort Wayne would be renewed. He beheld the advance Fort Wayne had made in manufactures with astonishment and pleasure, and with the progress he knew his own city was making, he was proud to lock hands with the citizens of Fort Wayne. He pledged himself to promote harmony between the two points. And Mr. Kinsey will do it. He is one of the live men of Cincinnati, who sees as he runs, what is best calculated to extend her prosperity.

He was followed by Mr. Biggs, of the Cincinnati Chamber of Commerce, who observed that fifty years ago the citizens of Cincinnati organized an expedition to explore this section of the country. Fifty miles from here they were met by hostile Indians, who forced them to retreat. "To-day," he playfully added, "we were met fifty miles from here, and captured by the Honorable Mayor and good citizens of Fort Wayne. In this instance, 'Barkis was willing.'" He then drew an interesting comparison between the old time way of doing business and the present, closing with the well expressed wish that the future success of Fort Wayne might equal the past.

By this time, the hilarity was so great, that Messrs. Turner, Jacobs, Greenwood, Bundy, and other gentlemen called upon, contented themselves with making a few remarks to the point.

His Honor then introduced to the assembly, "Mr. Loomis, the President of the Fort Wayne, Jackson & Saginaw Railroad."

That gentleman made a favorable impression. In the language of "the boards," he brought down the house. How could it be otherwise? The first words he spoke were a compliment to the might of the pen, and, of course, the press applauded. Then he invited us, in the most cordial manner, to take a ride with him in his humble coach the next day, and we cheered assent.

So ended the banquet, and with our hearts filled with good cheer, we bade good night to the citizens of Fort Wayne.

CHAPTER IV.

ON THE WAY TO JACKSON.

Wednesday morning, at 8 o'clock, our party assembled at the Saginaw depot, where a special train of palace cars, with superbly decorated engine "E. A. Webster" was in waiting. There, also, was the Jackson committee of invitation to receive us; Mr. P. B. Loomis, the President of the Fort Wayne, Jackson and Saginaw Railroad, Superintendent William A. Ernst, Hon. Eugene Pringle and Mr. E. A. Webster, Directors of same road, Mayor Noyes, City Attorney Peck, Recorder Tinker, Alderman Seaton and Messrs. Bennett and Knickerbocker.

Quite a number of citizens arrived to see us off, and the following named persons took passage with us:

Hon. F. P. RANDALL, Mayor, Fort Wayne.

Mr. T. S. TAYLOR, *Journal*, Fort Wayne.

Mr. JNO. J. GRAFTON and Wife, General Ticket Agent, Fort Wayne.

Judge R. LOWRY and Wife, Fort Wayne.

Miss ANNIE LOWRY, Fort Wayne.

Mr. F. S. SHURICK, Agent Associated Press and Correspondent *Cincinnati Gazette*, Fort Wayne.

Mr. W. T. JENISON, Fort Wayne.

Mr. WM. H. COOMBS and Wife, Fort Wayne.

Mr. WM. S. EDSALL, Clerk Allen County Court, Fort Wayne.

Mrs. E. P. EDSALL, Fort Wayne.

Mr. ROBERT G. MCNEECE, *Gazette*, Fort Wayne.

Mr. WM. B. HENDERSON, *Sentinel*, Fort Wayne.

Mr. W. B. WALTERS, *Sentinel*, Fort Wayne.

Miss LIZZIE M. EVANS, Fort Wayne.

Miss LIZZIE TOWNLEY, Fort Wayne.

Mrs. N. B. FREEMAN, Fort Wayne.

Taking our places in the cars there was a general interchange of felecitations, each excursionist flattering himself upon having been entertained by the most agreeable family in Fort Wayne. It must be confessed, not belonging to the itinerancy, that we had found ourselves assigned to private hospitality with a feeling of dust-and-travel-worn-unworthiness that was anything but pleasant—a feeling of intrusion, that, I am happy to say, was quickly dispelled by the gracious welcome we received.

Thus favorably impressed, the city looked beautiful to us that morning, and we left it with regret. The rain had washed every speck of dust from the houses and shrubbery, and they stood fair and fresh in the sunshine. The best view of the city must be from the Saginaw route, whence it lies high in the confluence of the St Joseph's and St. Mary's rivers.

Fairly under way, there are two prime objects of interest to the traveler; the conductor and engineer.

Assured at a glance that Mr. A. C. Smith could be relied on as cool, patient and capable, I gladly availed myself of an opportunity to make the acquaintance of the conductor.

Mr. Grafton introduced me to Mr. Webster. As a perfect stranger, Mr. Webster presented the *tout en semble* of a generous, whole-souled gentleman. He had an eye full of mischief, regular features, a pleasant smile and very engaging manners. He did not ask me if I was "anything to Vinnie Ream," but I at once remarked, "Was not the name 'Webster' on the engine?"

"My name," he replied, with pardonable pride. "Would you like to take a ride on the engine?"

"Of all things in the world," I answered. "Can you arrange it?"

"I think so," he quietly answered me.

Of course I did not know he was the young Jackson millionaire, and that the engine was named after him, and nearly belonged to him. Recognizing him only as a capital companion I followed along by the side of the train and climbed up into the cushioned, curtained and carpeted parlor of the engineer. Seated with others on either side of the engine, I was introduced to the engineer, whom I had abundant opportunity of observing. Standing by the engine with his hand on the throttle valve, Girard J. Shipman never took his eye from the track. The track stretched out to a point I could scarcely discern, while his accustomed eye was able to define objects at a great distance. Now he would ring the bell for a crossing, (there was a surprising number of them,) now whistle off something on the track, the engine going faster and faster as the wood was thrown in the furnace. What a hungry furnace it was, devouring the wood, both great and small, as it was thrown in! I hung my head out of the window and watched the piston, driving like mad, until I could reckon at what rate we were traveling, and the red wheels as they went round, seemed more beautiful than any dissolving views I ever witnessed. The feeling of exhiliration was indiscribable. It was greater than that of skating or riding on horseback. I felt, too, a sense of security unknown in the passenger coach, and a respect for the engineer hitherto beyond belief. With the motive power in his hand, he holds the lives of all on board at his will, and in the case

of Mr. Shipman, his care and vigilance proved him worthy
of the trust.

The weather, that 7th of June, was glorious. The rain
had dissipated the heat, the air was divine, and such a sky
was never seen before in summer! It was the clear blue of
azure, flecked and broidered heavily over with changing
white clouds, as in autumn. It was just the day for a ride
on a brand new locomotive, elegantly decorated with flags
and wreaths, through which her broad, brass sides shone
like burnished gold. It was positive rapture to watch her
bending her head to the work, and skimming along the iron
rails, the never so green earth on either side.

"But she's a beauty," I said to the engineer.

He did not turn his head or take his eye from the track,
but there was a glow of pride in his face as he said, "I tried
to make her look nice."

"Did you trim her up this fine way?" I asked in surprise.

"Every bit of it," he answered. ("There's one of my ban-
ners burning.) The ladies of Fort Wayne furnished the
wreaths of flowers; I did the rest."

"It was 'Ho for the wilderness!' in grand style," I thought
to myself, as we steamed along.

"Where's the wilderness?" I asked, as we made our way
through smiling villages and luxuriant farms. What a looney
I must have seemed to the engineer, who laughed, but made
no talk.

We drew up at Auburn, a little town by the way side, with
a very large school house, and I returned to the passenger
coach.

Our company here received the addition of Mr. P. C. Mays,
editor of *Courier*, Auburn, and his wife. The first act of this
enterprising gentleman was to pass around slips of paper
which read as follows:

"AUBURN,

County seat of DeKalb County, Ind. Situated on the Fort
Wayne, Jackson & Saginaw Railroad, and the present terminus of the Detroit, Eel River & Illinois Railroad. The line
of the proposed extension of the Baltimore & Ohio Railroad,

from Pittsburg to Chicago, will pass through this place. Population about 1,500."

Upon our return trip, Mr. Mays, as he left at this point, surprised us with a neat little speech, expressing his enjoyment of the trip, and venturing the hope that we would all meet again. It was received with great applause. One of my regrets in making up this work, is that I failed to receive his description of our trip; I know it would be vastly entertaining.

Waterloo was the next stopping place. Here we had the pleasant accession to our numbers of editor of the *Press*, B. F. Kennedy, and his wife.

Waterloo has a population of 2,000 and very considerable trade.

We next came to Pleasant Lake, situated upon a beautiful sheet of water by that name; thence to Angola, where the editor of the *Steuben Republican*, Mr. R. W. Weamer, and his wife, were added to our party.

Reading is the first village in Michigan on the line, and Jonesville is the point where the Lake Shore & Michigan Southern crosses. Here we were joined by Jos. J. Dennis, of *Independent*, Jonesville. At every one of these places the citizens were assembled at the depot, and greeted us with cheers and music by the band.

CHAPTER V.

FORT WAYNE, JACKSON AND SAGINAW RAILROAD.

It was during that ride from Fort Wayne to Saginaw, that I was furnished with the following interesting particulars of the Fort Wayne, Jackson and Saginaw Railroad.

Directors—P. B. LOOMIS, Jackson; H. H. SMITH, Jackson; D. MERRYMAN, Jackson; E. A. WEBSTER, Jackson; W D. THOMPSON, Jackson; W. R. REYNOLDS, Jackson; Hon. E. O.

Grovesnor, Jonesville; Hon. A. P. Edgerton, Fort Wayne; Henry J. Rudisill, Fort Wayne; A. H. Hamilton, Fort Wayne; John Bass, Fort Wayne; Henry Baker, Fort Wayne; Hon. James F. Joy, Detroit.

President, P. B. Loomis; Vice-President, A. P. Edgerton; Treasurer, B. S. Chapin; Secretary, Eugene Pringle; Attorney, J. D. Conely; Assistant Superintendent, A. H. Reese; Chief-Engineer, C. S. Woodward.

The road was inaugurated in form by the appointment of a committee of two, on the 24th of June, 1868, and organized in September, 1868, under the name of the Jackson, Fort Wayne & Cincinnati R. R. The Indiana portion of the line, known as the Fort Wayne, Jackson & Saginaw R. R., was organized in October of the same year. These two roads were consolidated on the 25th of February, 1869, under the latter name, and completed from Fort Wayne to Jackson, a distance of one hundred miles, in less than nineteen months, December 5th, 1870. The road, in its construction, has in all respects been made first class; its embankments being fifteen feet broad at the top, the cuts twenty-two feet in the bottom, and the slopes one-and-a-half to one; the sidings are numerous for a newly built road, and the road crossings well built. The income of the road has met the expenses, and the road is now prepared to do double the amount of former business, at very little increased cost.

It is of interest to know how so great a work was accomplished in so short a time. I have it from one who knows, that the committee, in order to inspire confidence in the communities through which the line projected, placed all the means raised in local districts at the disposal of the people of the district in which it was subscribed, permitting them to nominate the person as a local treasurer, who should have the entire charge of their contributions, to be paid out only on the certificate of the engineer of the company, and for work done in the vicinity wherein they resided or were interested. This is the way a body of men, scattered along a line difficult of intercommunication, were held firmly and persist-

3

ently to the accomplishment of a great work, at little expense, in a short space of time.

Considering the importance of the road as a link for the distribution of the products of the Saginaw Valley to the large area of country embraced in the States of Ohio, Illinois, Indiana, Missouri and Kansas, with eastern returns of freights of cattle, corn, etc., its future prosperity seems to be beyond a doubt.

The signs of habitation and agricultural wealth, increasing on either side of our route, showed us we were drawing near the city of Jackson. We were struck with the absence of suburban decay, which is part of even small places in old States. The transition was from the beautiful country to the beautiful town.

CHAPTER VI.

JACKSON.

It was high noon when we arrived at Jackson. The city lay near by to the left of the depot, and the street for a square or two was lined with elegant carriages and horses. We were met by the Committee of Reception: Mayor Noyes, City Attorney Beck, Alderman Loomis and Seaton, Recorder Tinker, Messrs, E. A. Webster, H. S. Ismon, W. M. Bennett, Eugene Pringle, W. D. Thompson, and C. R. Knicherbocker. These gentlemen took charge of us, assigning us to the carriages in waiting.

Our attention was at once drawn to the wonderful display of horses. They were beautiful, high-stepping and gay, with superb heads, planted firmly on proud, arching necks. And there was every variety to delight the eye—bay, black and grey, with an occasional roan and sorrel. In Mr. H. S. Ismon's carriage, I had the pleasure of riding behind two as handsome bays as ever trod the earth. They were large and strong, with glossy coats, and the fine qualities of limb and neck which are rarely seen in animals of their growth. They were simply perfect, and they were driven by a groom who knew all their good points by heart.

THE HOME OF MR. LOOMIS.

We drove first to the residence of Mr. Loomis. It is situated in a gently rolling wood, several acres in extent, and is approached by an irregular road nicely graded, and as smooth as the drives in Central Park. The house is many winged and of no particular style of architecture, having evidently undergone alterations and additions. A door here, a bay window there, to suit the present owner. To the right of the entrance is an elegant library, a large drawing room is on the left, half of one side of that opens into a charming boudoir, and that again is a wide detour to a snuggery, thus outlooking every point of the compass. The entire *suite* of rooms is elegantly furnished, most exquisite, pictures, statuary and books adorning the walls, niches, and nookies.

LOVELY OLD AGE.

In the boudoir there is an exquisite picture of an old lady. It looks from the canvass, large dark eyes of serenest depths, a holy calm about the lips, the face framed in by the soft lace border of a cap which falls over the forehead, and almost conceals the iron grey hair. It is the most charming picture of old age I ever beheld. It is the ideal type of a well spent life, crowned with scriptural peace and pleasantness.

I did not need to be told that it was the portrait of the mother of Mr. Loomis. I looked at him with new interest, and could discover in his face the same qualities of energy, fortitude and benevolence.

At his residence we enjoyed the charming hospitality of his wife and daughter, who were assisted in doing the honors by Mrs. Ernst, and other fair ladies of Jackson. Mrs. Ernst was noticeable for her lovely grey hair. It was less grey than black, and like Mrs. Greenwood's was worn in very becoming puffs. If I could describe Mrs. Greenwood and other ladies we met, and of our party, as they are impressed on my memory, it would be charming reading. It would also be a big book, and I must resume my story of our gay pilgrimage through Jackson to

THE CEMETERY.

After a drive through its beautiful grounds, we concluded that Jackson was not only a desirable place to live and die in, but the sweetest place on earth to be buried in. Having thus paid tribute to the dead of Jackson, we returned to the dwelling places of the living. Conspicuous among these was the

HOME OF MR. W. K. GIBSON,

another of the rich young men of Jackson. About the pleasantest feature of Jackson was the large number of rich young men. They must have the wisdom of age to have been able to make money, and they have youth to enjoy it. The distinction is plain. Mr. Gibson has a palatial mansion, with grounds like an English earl—a park and a lake; and what is better than all, he has an open, liberal heart. Long live he!

From Mr. Gibson's, again behind the trusty bays, we were driven through the town to

THE FAIR GROUNDS.

There is not generally much scenery about a Fair Ground, but this one had the most beautiful avenue of willows that can be imagined. The trees were fifty feet in hight, and their huge interlacing boughs formed a delightful arched way to the left of Grand River, two-thirds of the length of the grounds angling left to the race track.

The buildings of the Fair Grounds are well built and are kept in good repair, a man in charge living at the gate.

The races are a great attraction. The track is half a mile in length; but in view of the fact that Jackson is one of the best horse markets in the country, I was surprised to see so small a space for spectators; I should think not more than five thousand persons could view the track. We were there on the eve of a great Horse Fair, those well known champions of the turf, Lou Loder, Silas Rich and Pilot Temple having already arrived.

The next place we visited was

THE CHEMICAL WORKS.

It is chartered as the Michigan Chemical Company, and has a capital of $500,000. The main building is frame, its dimensions being 125 feet in length by 101 in width, with two shed roofs, above which rises a brick chimney 60 feet in hight, which serves as the escape pipe of three brick furnaces thirty feet square. There are several additional buildings, and the furnaces, boiling vats, cisterns, kettles and reservoirs are of vast proportions. The machinery is of most complicated and unique pattern.

The main object of attraction is a huge tower, built of stone slabs, seven feet square, and it is 70 feet to the summit of the tank which crowns its top. The tank contains a filterer, needed in the manufacture of chemicals. The articles manufactured are soda ash, sal soda, bicarbonate of soda, caustic soda, bleaching powder, chlorate of potash, and muriatic acid. The material necessary for the manufacture of these articles is found in abundance at and near Jackson.

It is the only establishment of the kind in the United States, or on the continent. Great Britain has hitherto monopolized the manufacture of soda, sal soda, or British soda, as it is called. Over a quarter of million tons of soda are manufactured annually, and when it is considered that two hundred tons per day are used in the United States, the importance of having established this branch of manufactures will be fully appreciated. It will also excuse my long account.

In the management of the chemical works, it was necessary to import some forty workmen from Europe, but already more than a hundred of our ingenious and ready countrymen have acquired the art. It is expected that 300 men will soon be employed.

Proposed weekly manufacture—70 tons soda ash, 50 tons soda chrystals, 50 tons bi-carbonate soda, 20 tons caustic soda, 40 tons black powder, which will consume weekly, 210 tons of salt, 580 tons of coal, 280 tons limestone, 40 tons Maganese ore.

MERCANTILE PROSPERITY.

In our short drive, we could see every indication of mercantile prosperity. The lumber yards, flouring mills and manufacturing industry are on a large scale. Of the last, the railroad shops are of marked importance. The work for five or six hundred miles of railroad is done here.

The Holly Water Works are in successful operation, as we can testify, who saw no less than five streams playing as high as a kite over Main street. This street, by the way, is handsomely built up and has a fine Nicholson pavement, and is plentifully dotted with gas posts.

Now said Mr. Ismon, I will take you to

MR. WEBSTER'S PLACE.

Driving to the western elevation of the suberbs, we entered the gate of a large oak clearing, elegantly laid off in walks and drives. We saw the site of Mr. Webster's new home, there is yet nothing but the foundation, but that looked large enough for a State House. The grounds are twenty acres in extent, and just hilly enough to give variety to the scene. What attracted observation was the novel shape of the grounds. To the east and south they were at a right angle, but west and north they had been dipped into in all manner of pocket-like shapes by lots, on which were built handsome dwelling houses, which gave them, (the grounds,) from a bird's eye view, the outlines of a Chinese puzzle. These houses, a hundred or more of them, in sight, were built by Mr. Webster to rent, but Jackson has so small a renting population, that they sold like hot cakes.

Through the north quarter of the grounds there is a rippling stream of water, which is fancifully bridged over. Crossing this, our party halted under a clump of trees, where a table was spread, and some finely dressed negroes served us with Champagne and Sandwiches. Such Sandwiches! Grated tongue in flakey biscuits, buttered when hot, and a sprinkling of mustard. The very thought of them is appetizing. No wonder, in the enjoyment of them, little master Benham, (the four year old of our party,) threw up his hat and cried: "How is this little thing for high?"

Here we had the additional happiness of making the better acquaintance of our fellow-excursionists and new friends, so that when dinner was in order, we sat down to it like the happy family in the full fellowship of brotherly love.

I can not say enough for a musical treat before dinner, to which we were indebted to the amiability of Mrs. Keating of Memphis, and Mrs. Lowry of Fort Wayne. They both sang with exquisite taste and feeling. Their sweet voices will live in our pleasantest memories. Mrs. Keating is a lovely blonde of the south, as graceful in bearing as refined and cultivated in mind; Mrs. Lowry is one of our Hoosier ladies. She is kind and fair and has a relish for social enjoyment which makes her the congenial friend of her charming *jeuenne belle fille.*

CHAPTER VII.

THE DINNER AT THE HIBBARD HOUSE.

After the bountiful collations at the houses of Messrs. Loomis and Webster, nothing short of the dinner at the Hibbard House could have tempted us. It was well cooked and well served, besides consisting of every conceivable delicacy and substantial dish.

We were seated at three long tables—two hundred and fifty of us in all. A reverend gentleman presided at one table, Mayor Noyes at the second, and Mr. Loomis at the third. At the drawing of the corks, Mayor Noyes arose, and pledging a toast of "welcome to our guests," called upon Mr. Loomis to reply. There was great straining of necks to see that gentle-

man when he got to his feet, and he was listened to with
unfeïgned delight. I can not begin to do justice to his speech
and the happy manner of it. It was as if, figuratively
speaking, he took each one of us to his heart in his friendly
welcome:

"*Ladies and Gentlemen of the Editorial Excursion to the Saginaw Valley:* I can not find words to describe the hearty
welcome the city of Jackson extends to you to-day. [Cheers.]
In welcoming you, members of the press, we do honor to the
highest power in the land—[Cheers again] a power superior
to kings and potentates, and mightier than a secret treaty
commission [Applause] or secret session of the Senate of the
United States. [Tremendous applause.] Recognizing you
as this power, we, the citizens of Jackson, beg leave to hope
that you will be favorably impressed with our little city.
[Cheers.] Again we welcome you, and trust we will meet
again." · [Cheers.]

Mayor Noyes then proposed "Louisville" as the first toast,
and called upon Mr. Converse to respond.

Now, Mr. Converse and his estimable lady were the veter-
ans of our party, and we looked for his remarks with respect-
ful attention. He is quite old and looks infirm—his delicate
features thrown in pale relief by his silvery hair. His manners are dignified but kind, and on our trip he had shown a
liberality of spirit worthy of imitation.

When called upon to speak, he rose as if he had scarcely
strength to stand, but his voice fell clear and strong on the
ear, as he expressed, in choice language, his appreciation of the
intelligence, enterprise and prosperity displayed in the city
of Jackson. In behalf of Louisville, he desired to extend
thanks for the courtesy and enlarged hospitality shown her
representatives. He jocosely observed that though weak and
feeble in his *personnel*, at least, they (the press) were *terrible*
with the pen, and should soon make due report of them. He
declared that on his return he would tell his children and his
grandchildren what he had seen and heard on this occasion,
and advise them to strive to emulate the enterprise and good
will of the people of Michigan, thus he would be doing his

part towards cementing a bond of union between the South and North stronger than the bands of iron that now united them. At the close of his remarks, there were hearty cheers.

To the second toast, "Michigan," Ex-Governor Blair responded in a pleasant voice and with an air of intelligence and *bonheur* which was very pleasing.

"It is but a little while," he said, "since we were strangers to those who lived fifty miles south of us, and we hail with delight the opportunity the railroads have afforded of taking counsel together. [Cheers.] I honor the press, and I have a great fear of editors. I have had occasion. [Laughter.] We welcome you to our city, [Cheers] and when next you come this way, we will take you by Houghten Lake to the Straits of Mackinaw and Duluth, the great center of creation, to Puget's Sound, the most beautiful sheet of water in the world, and thence to China, where Mr. Seward has gone to pave the way, and fit it, perchance, for annexation, as it lies contiguous to our northwest boundaries. [Great applause.] It will not be at a distant day either—this trans-continental route from pole to pole." [Cheers.]

This is scarcely an outline of Governor Blair's eloquent address, but I hope the spirit thereof is conveyed.

Here speech-making gave place to a song, "The Larboard Watch," from the "Appi Troupe."

To the third toast, "Tennessee,". Mr. Keating responded. In our brief acquaintance, he had impressed us as a thorough gentleman, of much culture and uncommonly keen powers of observation. When called upon to speak, he arose, and what with glowing face, sympathetic eye, deprecating words, and a certain indescribably touching timber of voice, he made a profound impression on the assembly. It was, perhaps, the first time that a full-blooded Southern man had had the ear of a Michigan audience. They listened to him with profound attention, if not critically, until finding the spirit they liked, they applauded without stint.

. I despair of being able to make anything like a correct synopsis of his remarks. The idea conveyed was:

"I never was more delighted in my life than on this trip.

We have been received with such whole-hearted, unbounded hospitality. And to say that I am surprised, does not express my amazement at the endless resources and enterprise of this section of the country. Surprised and delighted, I am prepared to believe that all that is necessary for the complete fraternization of the South and North is for them to get acquainted with each other. Neither one of us is as bad as we seem. [Applause.] As for Tennessee, [here his voice sank,] we are reconstructing very fast in the sense in which you have made a garden of the wilderness. Our city of Memphis was made as desolate as a wilderness by the war, but within the last two years we have been looking up again. Our population and trade are rapidly increasing and thriving. We now number 40,000 in population, and have handled in the last ten months no less than $120,000,000, and you can judge we have not had very much time to play the Ku Klux. We have rascals among us—[Laughter]—so have you; [More Laughter] but they are exceptions to the rule, and there is a difference which we would have you bear in mind. Every manner of crime with us is stigmatized as Ku Klux, while with you it comes under the head of police items. We have many serious obstacles to contend with, and we would ask you, before judging of us, "Put yourselves in our place." There is more than the mere name in that title of Charles Reade, "Put yourself in his place." It is the modern version of the divine rule of Christ "Do unto others as you would have others do to you." [Profound sensation.]

All in all, the South may congratulate herself upon having such representatives as Messrs. Keating and Whitmore, of Memphis, and Messrs. Turner and Converse, of Louisville. It was regretted that the attendance of the Southern press had not not been more general.

It is not unearthing dead issues to say that had the railway communication between the North and South been as complete as that between the East and West, there never would have been a war. There was no chance to put themselves in each other's places. Let the lines between the South and

North be drawn nearer, past the possibility of future misun-
derstanding.

But I am forestalling the excellent address of Mr. W. K.
Gibson, who responded to Mr. Keating's appeal, meeting him,
as the saying goes, more than half way. The spirit of his
generous words would be lost if I did not describe his personal appearance. At first glance I thought it was Mr. Webster. There was the same hearty manner, genial countenance,
and eyes of fun. As I have had occasion to remark before,
he is another of the young millionaires of Jackson, but there
isn't the shadow of a money line in his face; and it will not
do to say any more that riches harden the heart, with such
living contradictions as live and thrive in the city of Jackson.
The reader can imagine the enthusiasm infused by such words
as these:

"It gives me the heartiest pleasure to express, in behalf of
Jackson, our gratitude at the opportunity of welcoming you.
We would not welcome you with words only—our hearts are
open to you. If our Southern friends would welcome you
with open doors, *we will welcome you with our doors off their
hinges.* [Shouts of applause.] And when the editor of the
Memphis *Appeal,* in behalf of the South, comes half way, we
will meet him the other half, and be joined in a marriage so
strong, Chicago and all the politicians in America can not get
up a divorce between us." [Renewed applause.]

The speeches were diversified with music by the Appi Concert Troupe. Henri Appi sang "A man's a man for a' that,"
and when vociferously encored sang *Margery* with telling
effect. He is a great, burly fellow, and when the laugh came
in, he puffed out his cheeks and doubled up his body in the
most comical way. His laughter was infectious. We laughed
until we cried (no doubt it was very silly,) and then laughed
again.

To the toast of the Ladies, there was little verbal response.
The ladies had shown their appreciation by enjoying every
moment of our trip; and the best thing which can be said for
them is, that they did not interfere, in the least, with the
enjoyment of the Gilpins of our party. The man staid at

home who asked his friend, "Are you going to take your wife
along, or are you going to enjoy yourself?"

The regular toasts disposed of, Mayor Noyes introduced
Mayor Simoneau, of East Saginaw, who welcomed our party
to the hospitalities of his city, in the following words:

"*Gentlemen and Members of the Press Excursion:* The people of the young City of East Saginaw have delegated to me
and my associates here the pleasant duty of greeting you, and
extending in their name the hospitalities and courtesies due
to so distinguished a party of visitors. We come, gentlemen,
to bid you welcome to our pioneer homes, and proffer the
hand of friendship, and to exhibit the results that flow from
honest toil, and which are enriching us, and we hope in the
future will benefit you. We have no temples, but we have
curiosities of art and nature; and we have those other and
better things—a worthy people, and a productive industry
that ranks second to no other in our fair State.

"Such as we have, give we unto you; trusting these things
may be as pleasant in your sight as they are to us. The freedom of our city, of our homes, of our limits, shall be yours
while you sojourn in the Valley, and a kind remembrance is
all we shall ask in return; and to the gentleman of this sister
city who shall go home with us, we also say welcome, as
brethren in the heritage of the Michiganders.

"Without detaining you further, gentlemen, we say to all,
welcome to our Saginaw."

Mr. Hoschkins of East Saginaw Enterprise, followed in a
hearty speech of welcome to the "Southern friends."

Meanwhile there had been a play of wit between the parties at the second and third table, which I with others at the
first table was too far off to appreciate. At length "Mr.
Livermore" was called upon on the charge of being an
"abolitionist," and I saw a gentleman arise who would never
be called old, although he is white headed. His complexion
was as fresh as a rose, and his voice rung out crisp and cheery
as he said:

"I am a Jackson man, and yet the speaker calls me an
abolitionist. Why, sir, I was a Jackson man when the bears

and Indians swarmed through its streets. [Applause.] A few years ago I would have taken it as a great insult to have been called an abolitionist, but I am one now, and am proud of it. I would abolish all feeling of animosity between North and South, and I don't get mad very often, but when I hear the charge made that all our southern brethren are Ku Klux, I don't believe it, and as a Jackson man I repel the insinuation. [Cheers.] We welcome you with all the warmth of our affections. This city was named after General Andrew Jackson, and that is the kind of an abolitionist I am." [Applause.]

The banquet now partook largely of a love-feast, and there's no telling when it would have ended had not Mr. Webster announced that the cars were in waiting.

.

CHAPTER VIII.

JACKSON IN GENERAL.

Jackson is situated in the County of Jackson, which occupies the highest land in the lower peninsula, rivers running within its limits on the west to lake Michigan, and to lake Erie on the east. The face of the country is not diversified by hills, strictly speaking, but rather by high strips of land similar to the ridges between the valleys of high prairie land. The soil is very productive, being a rich, sandy loam. In mineral wealth the country is unsurpassed, having within easy reach large quantities of coal, iron, fire clay, marl and limestone. The timber is of the most valuable description. The small towns in the county are Grass Lake, Parma, Brooklyn, Napoleon and Concord.

Jackson lies on the Grand river, rising from the river in each direction to what might be called the upper basin of a valley terminus, which in turn, is overlooked by a high plateau, semi-circular in form, on which is located the cemetery and many beautiful residences.

Jackson is considerable of a railway center. There are no less than seven, radiating in different directions to the great iron ore deposits of the upper peninsula, the salt wells of Saginaw valley, the pine and other timber of north Michigan, and with eastern, western and southern lines of railroad, making Jackson the nucleus of all kinds of manufacture, and vast facilities for trade. Among the railroads completed are the Michigan Central, Grand River Valley, Michigan Air Line, Lake Shore and Michigan Southern, Jackson, Lansing and Saginaw, and the Fort Wayne, Jackson and Saginaw.

Forty years ago the country was a wilderness. Gov. Cass proclaimed it a seat of justice in 1831, under the name of Jacksonapolis (!) The main settlement of the county was in 1834–1837—about which time the State Prison was located here—but it grew slowly in 1841, being still yet unincorporated. The Central Railroad gave the first impetus to prosperity in 1841. By this time the name of Jacksonapolis was changed to Jacksonburgh. In 1843 the village was incorporated as Jackson, and it obtained a city charter in 1857. The population was then 3,000, which increased 1,000 in five years, (1860.) The population is now variously estimated at from 14,000 to 15,000, and the indications are favorable to doubling the census in the next five years.

There are twelve Churches, (two colored,) and ten secret and independent societies, by which are understood, Masonic, Odd-Fellows, and Temperance, Young Men's Christian Association and a Literary Society.

There are three flourishing newspapers and one job office:

The *Republican*, Werks & Van Dyne.

Daily and Weekly Citizen, James O'Donnel, publisher and Editor-in-Chief.

Daily and Weekly Patriot, Messrs. Carleton & Van Antwerp.

These are enterprising and entertaining journals, and are conducted by stirring, active, energetic business men.

Geographically considered, Jackson is 76 miles west of Detroit, 73 northwest of Toledo, 100 north of Fort Wayne,

100 south of Saginaw and 100 east of lake Michigan, to say nothing of being only 24 miles from the Magnetic Mineral Springs of Eaton Rapids, situated on the Grand River Valley division of the Michigan Central Railroad.

These springs were discovered in 1870, since which time, according to accounts, they have been visited by thousands of invalids, multitudes of whom have found in these waters a richer boon than gold can purchase—renewed health and vigor. Without detailing the analysis of the different springs, it is proper to say that they will cure every ill under the sun, and that the hotel accommodations are good.

CHAPTER IX.

THE JACKSON, LANSING & SAGINAW RAILROAD.

With the unexampled kindness shown us, as at Fort Wayne and Jackson, we begin to realize the meaning of the old saying, "carried on their hands." We were literally passed from the good hands of one corporation to another, and now surrendered unconditionally, to the delegation from Saginaw, consisting of the following gentlemen:

Mayor L. SIMONEAU, T. E. DOUGHTY, JEREMIAH FISHER, C. V. DeLAND, and J. G. HOTCHKISS.

The following gentlemen of Jackson accompanied us, and were also the guests of Saginaw:

Hon. J. S. NOYES, Mayor.

A. WATSON, Superintendent of the J. L. & S. R. R.

P. B. LOOMIS, President of the Fort Wayne & Jackson Railroad.

E. A. WEBSTER, one of the Directors of the above railroad.

H. S. ISMON, Merchant.

W. K. GIBSON, Lawyer.

C. D. WILBER, Merchant.

J. D. Van Dym, *Jackson Press*, and,

H. Pratt, Editor of the *News*, Mason.

At five o'clock, we took the train on the Jackson, Lansing, and Saginaw Railroad.

Directors.—Henry A. Hayden, Jackson; Daniel B. Hibbard, Jackson; W. D. Thompson, Jackson; H. H. Smith, Jackson; Peter B. Loomis, Jackson; O. M. Barnes, Mason; Minos McRoberts, Mason; W. H. Chapman, Lansing; N. Banard, Saginaw City; Thos. Merrill, Saginaw City; Henry W. Sage, Wenona; L. Westover, Bay City; Hon. J. B. Joy, Detroit.

Henry A. Hayden, President; Henry W. Sage, Vice President; O. M. Barnes, Solicitor and Secretary; W. D. Thompson, Treasurer; Andrew Watson, Superintendent.

Under charge of the above named officers, this road has rapidly increased in business during the past year. This is not shown as much by the receipts as by the amount of freight transferred, the company having reduced the rate of transfer, in order to compete with water transportation. The amount of property shipped by water out of the Saginaw Valley, is estimated at 80,000 car loads *per annum*. There is, besides, a very large quantity of ingoing freight. It is the object of this company (in conjunction with other railroad companies) to transport freight, in future, at prices better suited to the shipper, all things considered, than can be done by water.

The gross earnings of the road have increased at the rate of $100,000 annually, ranging now at between $600,000 and $700,000. The road is in excellent repair, and the above exhibit will show in a prosperous condition. Its extension to the Straits of Mackinaw, is under contract, and will speedily be accomplished. The wealth of the products, which this avenue will open to trade, can not be estimated. One third of the valuable pine lands of the Lower Peninsula of Michigan, the great lumbering streams of Pine, Rifle, Au Gres, Au Sable, Thunder Bay, and Cheboygan, and their branches, are entirely within it, as also parts of Tittabawassie, Muskegon, Manistee.

In this connection, by the Land Commissioners Report, it will be seen that the company is in possession of an extensive grant, amounting in all, to over half a million acres of land. Superintendent Watson did the honors of the road on this occasion, and if it were not so often misapplied, I could say, "won golden opinions" from every one. In short, we esteemed ourselves fortunate in being his guests.

As we drew near Lansing, we received a cordial invitation from her citizens to stop there over night, but as the programme for the morrow's entertainment had been arranged, we could not accept it. We tarried for a moment, and observed an inviting, well built town, with an immense building standing like a sentinel in the center. That, we were informed, was the Reform School, and is well worth a careful inspection.

It was night before we reached Saginaw, but there was light enough to distinguish a line of country, not unlike that of New Jersey, across from New York—marshy bottoms, and an even surface of ground, dotted over with a low growth of timber. We saw, too, a new style of architecture, in the shape of extensive low buildings, that were not quite like a brewery, and yet did not look like a slaughter house or distillery. They certainly did not have the odor of these familiar nuisances. These buildings were surrounded with a trestle work, on which were placed immense vats, from the sides of which oozed a brackish looking white substance. We might have known they were salt mills, or "salt blocks," if we had for a moment realized the importance of this branch of industry—salt blocks they were, and I shall have occasion to speak of them again.

CHAPTER X.

THE PRESS OF SAGINAW.

Within a few miles of Saginaw, each member of our party was handed an envelope containing a double slip elegantly inscribed with:

4

The Press Gang of Saginaw Valley to the Members of the Newspaper Fraternity from the South and South West: "Welcome." Editorial Excursion to Saginaw Bay, June 6th and 9th, 1871.

Newspapers.

Daily and Weekly Courier, East Saginaw, Dem., C. B. Headley, Editor, G. W. Hotchkiss, Associate Editor and Business Manager.

Daily and Weekly Enterprise, East Saginaw, Rep., G. W. Fish, Editor, G. W. Cameron, Associate Editor, T. B. Fox, City Editor.

Saginaw Zeitung, East Saginaw (German,) Ind., C. Brierle, Editor.

Saginawian, Saginaw City, Weekly, Dem., Geo. F. Lewis, Editor and Proprietor.

Republican, Saginaw City, Weekly, F. A. Palmer, Editor and Proprietor.

Chesaning Times, Ind., Weekly, W. P. Allen, Editor.

Herald, Wenona, Weekly, Rep., J. B. Ten Eyck, Editor and Proprietor.

Journal, Bay City, Tri-weekly and Weekly, Rep., R. L. Warren, Editor and Proprietor.

Chronicle, Bay City, Weekly, Ind., J. Birney, Editor and Proprietor.

Nine newspapers—two of them dailies. This did not look much like the wilderness, and when next morning we were each furnished with a copy of these papers before breakfast, we rather inclined to the opinion that we had arrived at the head center of civilization. They were printed on clear type, on handsome paper, and contained, besides an unusual amount of intelligence, a surprising number of valuable advertisements, and vigorous, well written, spicy editorials. What struck us, particularly, was the enthusiasm with which we were greeted. It was very flattering, and, at the same time, overwhelming. We felt that we were made more of than we deserved—a feeling which, I may say here, increased every moment of our stay, until we absolutely flew in the face of extended courtesies by running away. We knew that if we owned a bank, and lived a thousand years we could never return the thoughtful, high-handed kindness of the citizens of Saginaw Valley.

As for the press, the leading columns were headed "Welcome," and because I can give no idea of their distinguished courtesy, I transcribe the one from the *Enterprise:*

"*Welcome to our Editorial Brethren and other distinguished Guests:* It is with a genuine feeling of pleasure that we join with the citizens of Saginaw in welcoming our distinguished visitors who arrived in our city last evening from Jackson. That we should be thus favored we hail as a fortunate circumstance, and we indulge the hope that to us, as a people, the associations of to-day will not soon be forgotten by either. The people of this country have long since recognized how powerful an agency is involved in the Press—how vast an influence it is exerting on the destiny of the world, and we are satisfied whatever honor is bestowed upon our editorial and other visitors to-day, will be in accord with that generous hospitality for which Saginaw is noted.

"Our editorial brethren, and those accompanying them, may rest assured they are in good hands, among a people who would like to keep you a longer time than you feel at liberty to stay. We trust your sojourn among us will be one of pleasure, and that you will see many things in your visits to-day which will be of interest to you, and perhaps valuable to you in the future."

Was not that enough to quite take our breath?

CHAPTER XI.

SAGINAW.

We did not talk any more about the wilderness; but with the press card before us, we yet did not realize that there was more than one local habitation under the name of Saginaw. We arrived at a depot after night, where half of us were dropped, the rest to go on—to East Saginaw, we were told.

We were to be quartered in Saginaw City, a mile and a half this side. Two Saginaws!—we made a note of that in our mind. We were assigned to the Taylor House, Saginaw City, and our other friends at the Everett and Bancroft, in East Saginaw. "All of them first class, but the Taylor House is kept by Mr. Hopkins, an old Indianapolis gentlemen." That is what was said in the cars, and the last clause of the sentence decided our part of the party. With the old notion of the wilderness clinging to us, we wended our way to the Taylor House—it is but a step from the Depot. What was our astonishment to find a five story building, whose outlines were dimly but beautifully defined in the starlight. It is built of the cream colored brick peculiar to Saginaw, and has iron columns, cornice, and window caps painted lake color, a favorite style of finish in this locality. We entered a broad staircase, catching a glimpse of marble floors in the office and halls; and a spacious dining room, and ascended to the second floor, where we were ushered into an elegant drawing room. To the end of the hall was a superb verandah (room for four,) from which we looked out on city like buildings, looming up against the leaden sky, and listened to music from the band, which fell on the ear very sweetly as we sniffed the breeze from the lake. That breeze was so pure, so fresh, without a bit of a draught to take cold in—oh, it was delightful! And the land-lubbers we were, we could not believe it would last; though the same blessed air came through our lattice all night, and we slept the sleep of comfort and content.

But before we slept, we had an excellent supper; and before we eat the supper, we had another welcome—this time from a scholarly looking individual, who, I was informed *sotto voce*, is a very talented and thriving young lawyer, Mr. Hanchett. He welcomed us in an admirable address, in behalf of the Mayor, Common Council, and citizens of Saginaw City, to which Mr. Jacobs, of Indianapolis, (dropping his fork,) responded on the part of our part of the party, in a peculiarly felicitous manner. The form of welcome over, we made it practical by social enjoyment, and by partaking heartily of the good things spread before us. A similar welcome was extended to the guests of the Bancroft and Everett Houses. By way of parenthesis, let me say that in these fine hotels of Michigan, we were favored with the rare sight of a landlord, and I can not describe the satisfaction it added to being well cared for.

After breakfast, we found a deputation of citizens waiting in carriages to convey us over the city, or cities. Our first care was to learn their geography. There were Saginaw City and East Saginaw, with the adjacent villages of Florence, Carrolton, and South Saginaw, comprising in all a population of $25,000 souls. The Saginaw river runs between the Saginaws, and is crossed by three substantial draw-bridges, the street cars running from one town to the other. The river is navigable for vessels not drawing over eleven feet of water, and is seventeen miles in length, taking its rise in the junction of the Cass, Shiawassee, and Titabawassie rivers, just above East Saginaw.

The trade of the Saginaw river is estimated at $20,000,000 a year.

These figures sounded as vague to me as the distance of the sun from the earth, but I could not disguise my astonishment at the evidences of wealth and refinement on every side. There was particular taste displayed in the dwelling-houses. In

EAST SAGINAW,

There must be fifty elegant houses facing on the proposed city park, and located in pleasant groves of oak timber. The park grounds will admit of picturesque cultivation, stretching along a ridge of high ground on the street, and sloping down unevenly to the low lands of thicket and marsh. The marsh can be drained into a lake of enchanting loveliness.

East Saginaw claims to be the commercial center of the valley, being the seat of the State Salt Inspector's office, and of the Saginaw Valley Lumberman's Association. It has many fine blocks of houses, is lighted with gas, and has miles of brick sewerage. It has two street railways, a brick skating rink, public halls, Nicholson pavements, and all the necessary belongings of a live, thriving city. From the cupola of the Bancroft House, "the great lumber exchange of the Valley," can be counted the tall stacks of thirty-five saw mills, nine shingle mills, and thirty salt blocks, all in active operation. There are eight churches, and the school property of this and Saginaw City is greater in value, in proportion to the number of children, than in any other town in Michigan. Its present population is 13,000; in 1850 it was 17. It supports two daily and three weekly newspapers, including the *Zeitung*, a German paper.

The Bancroft House, strange to say, was about the first house built. The story goes: it is

A SAGINAW LEGEND:

That a certain rich man in New York owned a large tract of wild land in these parts. He rejoiced also in the paternity of a wild son. The son was very wild, indeed, and to give him an opportunity of sowing his wild oats, his father sent him out to look after his wild land. Now, there wasn't any thing so very bad about the young man. He was only running to waste for something to do, and when he spied the land, there was enough of his father's son in him to see there was money in it. He set to work improving the land. He built a hotel. He built the Bancroft House right in the woods, and hired somebody to keep it. He built houses, and if he did not exactly hire people to live in them, he gave them money to live on and set them up in business. In a little while, East Saginaw was a bustling, thriving place, and the wild young man a rich young man on his own account. You may be sure, when the news of it came to the rich father in New York, he rejoiced greatly, and in a short time he died, and his son entered upon his inheritance. And—that is the end of my story.

Moral: His name was Hoyt.

SAGINAW CITY.

This is the oldest settlement in the Valley and has a population of 10,000. A trading post was established here and a fort built for its protection as early as 1812. It became an important fur trading point in 1836, when vessels began plying between it and Detroit. It was then known as Pontiac, but eventually took the name of Saginaw, which, in the Indian dialect, means "a place to camp." It is now a handsomely built and substantial city. It can boast of a grand hotel, the Taylor House, and of a splendid Union School building. In the general distribution of splendid school buildings, I do not need to give its length and breadth, but I wish I had space to describe the best jail in the North West. A clean, well ventilated, wholesome jail is such a rarity in this Christian land, that the citizens of Saginaw should have credit for one. I might almost call it a cheerful jail. And it is not expensive either. I commend its plan to county commissioners.

But the main object of our drive was to see

THE SAW MILLS AND SALT BLOCKS.

It was not necessary to inform us that we had arrived at the region of lumber and salt. There were saw mills to the right and to the left of us as far as the eye could reach. There were booms of logs on either side of the river and up the streams emptying into it were logs by the millions—"at least one hundred and fifty miles of logs," I was told, waiting their turn to be sawed.

I do not know if it would last, but for the time, there was something very attractive about the lumber business. Perhaps because these Saginaw people were so liberal we have formed an idea that business fosters generosity and manliness. It seems of interest, from the felling of trees in winter to the freshets which, by the aid of the log masters, carry the nicely marked logs to their respective owners. The wood choppers find employment at the mills and salt works in summer. Mr. Chapin pointed one out to me. He was engaged in supplying the saw with logs. It was a curious study to watch him engineer them in position, when, by pulling a rope, the truck would suddenly emerge from the water and, with the logs securely spiked, run up the track as if it was a monster alive and had shouldered the helpless lumber. The engineer, meanwhile, steadily ascending at the side, shortening the rope hand over hand, until the load is dumped and the car runs down, like mad, for another brace of logs. The hungry mill sawing them as fast as they could be carried up.

It was the pleasantest study of all to see the labor saving machinery and the readiness with which the foreman decided the uses of a log—whether it was to make common or choice lumber, and the size thereof. There were men at hand to seize the lumber and dispose of the scantlings, stickings and slabs—the largest of the latter were cut into staves, the refuse made fuel of, or, with saw dust, converted into piers and town lots.

"You will see the gang saws at work in Bay City. They will be worth seeing," Mr. Chapin said to me. I had no idea what he meant, but I was ready to believe them worth seeing.

I could write a chapter on the uses of saw dust and slabs. Passing through the engine room, I found saw dust was used as fuel. "We saw enough," Mr. Chapin said, "to run the saw mill during the day and keep the salt works going day and night." He then showed me a wooden frame to an iron tube which conducted the steam from the saw mill to the salt works. Before we visited them, I took a peep into the furnace to see

A SAW DUST FIRE.

There it was, a bank of saw dust reduced to what looked like a huge honey comb at white heat, clouded over with red drifts from the many colored, beautiful flames which continually burst from the fresh, smoking saw dust as the fireman shoveled it in. Does any of my fellow excursionists recognize the picture?

LOT'S WIFE.

The salt works were an object of greater curiosity, if not interest, than the saw mills. We visited three varieties engaged in the manufacture of salt by steam, furnace and solar heat. It was then we learned the uses of the long sheds, high vats and brewery shaped buildings. We certainly were never in cleaner places, while the air was delightful. The salt looked as beautiful as it is savory, piled up in the bins or in the dripping baskets. As we threaded our way around carefully, a youth of our company said to Mrs. Greenwood:

"How would you like to be turned into a pillar of salt like Lot's wife?"

"I would not care," she replied, "if I could be as pure as this," holding up to his view an exquisite salt crystal, which had been presented to her.

No preachment was intended, but the words, fitly spoken, sank into every heart.

The salt wells at Saginaw are considered the best in America, containing a larger quantity of salt of purer quality. No less than 645,576 barrels were manufactured during the year 1870.

A WOMAN'S NOTE.—To make the grain of the salt fine, a certain quantity of butter is used.

CHAPTER XII.

DOWN THE VALLEY.

The next thing in order was the visit to Wenona and Bay City. Here our party divided—a portion going down by rail and the rest on the steamer Minnie Bell, by water. All the way, seventeen miles, the river was lined with saw mills, salt works, and log booms; the water being a deep chocolate hue from the last. The border-land was low and marshy, and abundantly anchored with saw dust and slabs.

Arrived at Bay City, we visited Mr. Brewer's mill, which, in the distance, we mistook for a fashionable watering place. Its entire cost, including engine, was $150,000. All the work about the mill is done by machinery. This mill has two gang saws, with eighty-seven saws in each gang, besides one large circular saw, two slabbing saws, and several small circular saws. The yearly capacity of this mill is 25,000,000 feet. A few feet distant from this building is "a salt block," as salt works are called. Some of the wells here are eighteen hundred feet in depth. Between seven and eight hundred barrels of salt are manufactured a week.

We also visited the mill of H. W. Sage & Co., at Wenona, which has the largest capacity of any mill in the Valley. Not long ago it sawed 370,797 feet in twelve hours.

GANG SAWS AT WORK.

Talk about pageants and spectacles! I can not imagine a much finer sight than two mighty gang saws, each one crashing a fourteen feet log into boards in a minute and three-quarters, sixty strong; neatly clad men in attendance! It was somewhat noisy, but it is the music which has rung to the wealth and honor of the Saginaw Valley. This is the measure of 1870: $16,275,725.

After the visit to the mills, we took passage on the steamer Eighth Ohio, Capt. Burrington, and were transported out to the Bay and back. It was a pleasant trip, enlivened by music and brief, racy speeches.

BAY CITY

Was another vast surprise. Think of it. An Opera House worth $100,000, in the wilderness, (but I believe I was not to speak of that any more,) a hotel on as grand a scale, banks with half a million of capital, eight school houses, (one worth $6,000,) and the biggest saw mill in the world! There is a manufactory of wooden water and gas pipes in successful operation, with a capital of $200,000.

Here, again, we were impressed with the enterprise and urbanity of the press. Under their safe convoy, we proceeded to the Fraser House to partake of the

GRAND PRESS EXCURSION DINNER,

On *Thursday, June 8th*, 1871, *at the Fraser House, Bay City, Michigan.*

Soups.—Mock Turtle; Tomato.

Fish.—Boiled Saginaw Trout, Egg Sauce; Boiled White, Butter Sauce.

Cold Dishes.—Beef Tongue; Sugar Cured Hams; Corned Beef.

Boiled.—Beef Tongue; Chicken with Pork; Corned Beef; Bertch Sugar Cured Ham; Leg of Mutton, Caper Sauce.

Roast.—Rib of Beef, Brown Sauce; Pork, Apple Sauce; Spring Chicken, Giblet Dressing; Spring Lamb, Mint Sauce; Spring Pig, Apple Sauce; Ham; Mutton; Veal.

Entrees.—Sweetbread Panne Aux Petits Poix; Tenderloin of Beef, Larded Mushroom Sauce; Roast Ham, Champagne Sauce; Calf Head, Brain Sauce; Boiled Buffalo Tongue, Tomato Sauce; Fricassee Chicken, with Fine Herbs.

Vegetables.—New Beets; Sweet Corn; Stewed Tomatoes; New Onions; Boiled Potatoes; Green Peas; Hominy; Rice; Turnips; Mashed Potatoes.

Relishes.—Tomato Catsup; Worcestershire Sauce; Cumberland Sauce; London Club Sauce; Radishes; Mushroom Sauce; Walnut Catsup; Plain Pickles; Lettuce; Olives; Scullions; Assorted Pickles.

Pastry and Desert.—Cherry Pie; Lemon Pie; Rhubarb Pie; English Plum Pudding, Brandy Sauce; Rice Pudding, Plain Sauce; Currant Cake; Silver Cake; Jelly Cake; Cocoanut Cake; Marble Cake; Pecans; Almonds; Brazil Nuts; Filberts; Coffee; Oranges; Strawberries; Lemon Ice Cream; Sponge Cake; Vanilla Ice Cream.

Any one will admit that this was a dinner fit to set before the king, but our party unwittingly put Messrs. Van Dusen and McClain to some inconvenience. Each and every one called for fish. Some of us waited for it to be caught and cooked.

"I did not count," said one of the proprietors, "on many wanting fish this hot weather."

"Just bear in mind, then," a gentleman replied, "we Southerners always want fish."

He hailed from about Muncie, but we were all Southerners to the people of Saginaw.

The substantial viands disposed of, we were served with sparkling Catawba, and it is high time for me to say that, with all the flow of wit and wine, there was no intoxication.

There were a few members of our party who did not drink
any, and those who did, kept within the bounds of decorum.

Judge Birney of the *Chronicle*, presided with much grace and
dignity. He is a courteous, high-bred gentleman, good looking withal, but he has a certain air of the city which made us
wonder how he ever escaped from Cincinnati. Rising tó his
feet, he said, in his courtly way:

"Bay City is proud to welcome this excursion party, com-
posed, as it is, of persons of distinction and wide influence,
who may go from our midst to convey to their readers and
friends an assurance of the activity and wealth which they
find in our city and valley.

"I see many before me from Cincinnati, of which (my old
home) I cherish the most pleasant recollections. I was back
there on a visit recently, and they asked me where I was living. I informed them, at Saginaw. 'Saginaw, Saginaw.
Where is Saginaw?' they said. [Laughter.] Now, some of
them will know. The truth is, most of the people in the
South do not recognize such a place as Saginaw on the map
of the American Continent; but those of you who are here
now, can return and tell their people of Saginaw prosperity
and enterprise." [Cheers.]

Col. C. V. Deland here extended, on behalf of the F. & P.
M. Railway Company, an invitation to those who should
choose to remain and take a trip over the newly opened sections of their road.

Judge Birney then proposed the first toast: "Cincinnati,
Muncie and Fort Wayne linked with Bay City with iron
bands."

Mayor Randall, of Fort Wayne, responded. He said he was
happy to be called upon to respond to such a toast. He would
take this opportunity of again reminding those that had heard
him on a previous occasion, that there was a great North, and
asked them to look to that North, which was being rapidly
developed. He was one of those who believed this excursion
would do much good. The people of Fort Wayne were
anxious that the people of Cincinnati, Louisville and other
places South, should learn that there was a direct line from

Fort Wayne to the Northern Lake. This excursion would be advantageous to all alike, and it was for all to form mutual acquaintances from the Ohio river to this place. The cities of the South and South West wanted your lumber, and such occasions would be mutually beneficial. Commerce would follow these kindly associations, and Fort Wayne and Bay City would soon be bound with an iron band.

The next toast: "Ohio: her Cincinnati, the Queen of the West."

Dr. Comegys, of Cincinnati, responded. He expressed in glowing language his astonishment at the prosperity and enterprise of the Saginaw Valley, and words failed him to convey his appreciation of the courtesies he had received. In behalf of Cincinnati, he begged leave to hope that the fellowship between her and the Saginaw Valley, thus happily begun, would be kept alive and strengthened in the future.

Judge Birney then asked to hear from Mr. Miles Greenwood, of Cincinnati. Now, there had not been an industry or entertainment which had escaped the study and deliberation of this estimable gentleman, and his response naturally hinged on enterprise. There was so much cheering that it was impossible to catch all he said, but the meaning was clear. There can be no enterprise where there is no money. Money is prosperity: without prosperity there can be no enterprise. It is like trying to make bricks without straw. [Applause.]

Mr. Greenwood paid a forcible tribute to the paying enterprise of the Saginaw Valley, and concluded with a toast, which was received with deafening cheers: "The Ladies: God bless them!"

Mr. Biggs, in behalf of the Cincinnati Chamber of Commerce, returned thanks for courtesies, and pledged a return a hundred-fold. [Cheers.]

The next toast: "The Ladies: their influence moulds the Press, the Press the Nation."

Judge Lowry, of Fort Wayne, responded; "I am wholly at a loss what to say in addition to what has been already said. I am not the handsomest man in the company, and was not the proper person to respond to this toast. Perhaps

I was called upon because in my legal practice I have acquired some fame in the defense of criminals; and who are greater criminals than thieves, and who greater thieves than the ladies, who so persistently steal our hearts? I am glad to arise in their defense.

"Burns has said that Providence,

> 'His 'prentice hand first tried on man,
> And then he made the lassies.'

> 'Oh, woman, in our hours of ease,
> Uncertain, coy, and hard to please;
> But when in pain and sore disease,
> A ministering angel these.'

"First at the tomb as last at the cross, so first in all good to our race. Much of the prosperity of this Valley is due to the energy inspired by the devotion and regard for wives and daughters.

"In conclusion, I will offer the following toast: 'The Ladies of Saginaw Valley: beautiful, and worthy to be the wives of such intelligent and enterprising husbands.'" Received with great applause.

The next toast was "Kentucky—the blue grass region—famous for all that is lovely;" to which Mr. Converse responded briefly.

He was not accustomed to speaking, but he had been a writer for almost half a century, and it would be his pleasure to chronicle all what was in his power of the enterprise, kindness and liberality of the Saginaw Valley.

Mr. Rogers, of the Continentals, now sang "The Sword of Bunker Hill," which was received with a noisy *encore*.

Judge Sutherland, of East Saginaw, was called upon to answer to the toast of "Our Sister Cities," which he did with a number of local hits. They must have been very funny, for to us, who did not understand them, it was as amusing as any pantomime we ever saw. A citizen explained that there was considerable rivalry between the Saginaws and Bay City, although the prospect was fair that they would some day become one.

The next toast: "Tennessee: her cotton and her enterprise make her among the first of the States."

Response by Mr. Keating.

Mr. Keating said, in the presence of the manufacturers of Saginaw, he had but little to say in behalf of the manufacturers of Tennessee. After all I have seen, I much wish that all my friends South could see what I have seen for the past few days. We of the South are prospering, and as we recover from the depression into which we have been plunged, we hope to welcome you to our purified and ennobled homes. [Applause.] We have formed new ideas of your people, and shall gladly welcome you whenever you can visit the South. The speaker closed with a high eulogy upon the citizens of Saginaw Valley for the warm reception they had accorded to their guests from the South. Mr. Keating was warmly applauded, but he was not as much at his ease as when he spoke in Jackson. He told a gentleman privately, that when it came to speaking of the enterprise and kindness of the Saginaw people, he gave it up. He could not do justice to the subject.

To the next toast—"The Press: all powerful for good or ill, its freedom and the liberties of the people are one and inseparable"—Mr. Robert McNiece, editor of the Fort Wayne *Gazette*, responded. A fitter representative could not have been chosen. He brings to the profession scholarly attainments, and a keen perception of the active, living present He is modest withal, and in his remarks seemed to labor under much embarrassment.

Mr. McNiece said: "Please accept my hearty thanks for all the courtesies displayed toward the members of the press on this occasion, as I know each one would gladly do so in person, could he express his individual feelings. After the silver cake from Memphis, and the cocoanut cake from Saginaw and Bay City, I should be like the man who swallowed the cake, and then took a bitter pill. I leave you to make the application. I am not the one to be called upon at this point of the feast. [Yes, yes, yes.]

"In this advanced age it is not necessary to speak of the

influence of the press. It is said that the London *Times* was instrumental in causing the Crimean war, and there is no religious or civil reform which could not be realized to-day with a united press. [Applause.]

"Editors need to travel, and they will find that they are not the only cabbage heads in the world. Horace Greeley, no doubt, has been thought by many of the South to have horns, but they have found that he was as much like a man as any other man, if he *was* the poorest speaker they ever heard. [Laughter.]

"We have learned on this trip that there are some other important places in the world beside Chicago. We have learned that, in order to get to some important places in this country, it is not absolutely necessary to get there by the way of Hades, or Chicago." [Cheers.]

This is, of course, but an imperfect transcript of remarks, which, delivered in a clear, musical voice, had a pleasing effect.

One of the ladies expressing a desire to hear from Judge Sutherland, on the home topic of "East Saginaw." The mere recital of his words can give no idea of his oratory. It is not what he says so much, as his manner of saying it, and he holds a master hand over the sympathies of his audience:

"We, of the cities of the up river, feel grateful for the kind sentiment expressed in the term sister. We are glad to feel that we have the sympathy of our brother at the head of lake navigation. We ask the privilege of visiting you occasionally in our canoes. You may, by and by, be visited by the calamity of railroads, centering in Bay City. We will do nothing to avert the calamity from you. We still ask you to sympathize with us in the spring, when we have too much water, and, as now, when you think we have too little. We are glad to mingle with you on such occasions as the present, and trust these fraternal courtesies may bind us in a closer band of union."

Now we had the happiness of seeing and hearing the irrepressible Hotchkiss, of the East Saginaw *Enterprise*, on his own ground. I alluded to his speech at Jackson.

The toast to which he responded was, "Michigan, my Michigan."

My sentiments are in common with the poet, who asked—

> "Lives there a man with soul so dead
> Who never to himself hath said
> This, my own, my native land."

"As citizens of Michigan, we look with pride upon our fair State and its immense resources. Rich in all things conducive and necessary for the welfare of our State, or of our sister States, we welcome our visiting friends to our midst that they may learn what we have, to furnish them of those things which will add to their prosperity and welfare, and we are glad to learn from them of their desire for closer relations with us. We have resources, how great, we do not know ourselves, and if our guests woud stay with us a month, we would, in our already developed resources, and in those we are daily developing, display new wonders each day, and show you new branches of industry which we can offer in trade to our Southern brethren. We are glad to welcome you, our friends, to our State and Valley; and we trust the results of this occasion will cement in a closer bond of union with us, those to whom in the past we have been comparatively strangers, and lead to better acquaintance and more extended relations. The time is near at hand when we will invite you to go over our roads to Mackinac, thence to Duluth, the far-famed city, the center of the universe; thence to Puget Sound, the most beautiful water in the world; thence to China, where Mr. Seward is now negotiating for annexation, in order that, embracing all the elements of greatness, we may prove ourselves what we aspire to—the greatest nation upon which the sun ever shone." [Cheers.]

Thus ended the banquet, and with parting benisons on the Happy Valley, we took the cars for Saginaw.

SHA-BE-NEE-GANSE.

This is the name of the Indian who was invited to accompany us on the excursion to Bay City and Winona. He is the son-in-law of Naw-Chic-a-mee, the present chief of all the tribes in that part of the country. The chief is now over ninety years of age, but has retained all his faculties, and can relate thrilling experiences and observations in the history of his race. There is but a remnant of them left, and they have been deprived, by all manner of foul means, first of their birthright, and then of subsidies from it. The Isabella Grant is now the largest and most valuable of their possessions, and what speaks ill for their nationality, it has been retained, as much in spite of them as of the white citizens, an Indian having done his best to traffic it away.

The Indian of our party, Sha-be-nee-ganse, is an exception to the general rule of indifference to pecuniary matters. He is the owner of a fine farm, and by his industry, thrift and honesty, has commended himself to the good graces of the Valley people. He frequently joins them in hunting excursions, and is of infinite service. The Indians have a passion for the circus, and in not being at Saginaw Thursday afternoon, we missed an opportunity of seeing them in full force, pappooses and all.

Sha-be-nee-ganse was accompanied by his son, whose name sounded quite like Ginger-snaps, meaning in the Indian dialect "Big man." His father's name signifies "needle," and he calls himself David, but is generally known as Sha-be-nee-ganse. He is a very likely specimen of the Lo family, but would not be considered at all handsome. He is tall, and moves with a graceful, elastic, onward tread that can not be imitated, but his eyes are small, his head ill shaped, his cheek bones are too high and prominent, and there is a sinister expression about his lips. In conversation he is retiring and frank. This is his tribute to the press:

"White man has more sense than Indian. White man write down what he knows in a book. White man has it. Indian put it down in his head. Indian forget it."

Sha-be-nee-ganse was attired in a semi-barbaric manner, which rendered the half civilized raiment becoming. On his head he wore a fur turban, surmounted by a crown of eagle plumes, as big as the moon. His coat was black broadcloth, but it was of the finest texture, and belted in with an embroidered girdle, hung with deer hoofs, eagle claws, and fanciful shells. Crossing over the left shoulder, under his right arm, was a band of leather, upon which was neatly mounted the skin of a rattlesnake, complete from head to tail point, to which last was suspended a number of lively rattles. He was very generous with these trophies, distributing them around to any one who expressed a wish for them. His nether trappings were the marvel. Short clothes, or breeches of black broadcloth, with a six inch border of exquisite bead work—elaborate design on field of scarlet—falling over the knees, and meeting superb Huzzar shaped leggings. The moccasins were beautiful specimens of needle-work, and outlined feet a dainty girl might envy.

Such was the holiday dress of Sha-be-nee-ganse, and it was scrupulously neat. The only thing to mar its grace, was a paper collar, which was worn a size to small.

RE-UNION AND SERENADES.

As if enjoyment enough had not been crowded into the day, we were invited to attend a citizens' reception and promenade concert, at Irving Hall, East Saginaw, Thursday evening, June 8th.

We found an assembly of five or six hundred people, in an elegant hall, splendid music, and a profusion of flowers and delicacies. The enjoyment I have not words to describe. Some of our party were dancing at two o'clock in the morning. Mr. Greenwood knows who they were.

At home, some time in the morning, we were soothed to rest by a serenade from Prof. Barnhardt's celebrated cornet band.

CHAPTER XIII.

THE SAGINAW VALLEY.

I have endeavored to convey what scraps of information I picked up as much in the palatable form of "object lessons" as possible, but I must be allowed a brief resume of the geography and statistics of the Saginaw Valley.

I have shown how the Saginaw cities are located on either side of the Saginaw river, flanked by the villages of Carrolton, Florence, and South Saginaw. With the saw mills, salt blocks and log booms, the population is continuous a distance of seventeen miles to Winona and Bay City. At these points it is yet ten miles to the Bay proper, and from this harbor · vessels are constantly leaving, loaded with timber and salt for all quarters of the globe.

The productions of the Valley are limited only by the number and capacities of the producers—the resources are unlimited.

The business of the Valley is set down at $20,000,000 a year. The division of products is timber, $16,275,725, salt, $1,300,000, and the remainder in fish and manufactures.

The salt wells were not discovered until 1860, and the product is greater than that of the Onandaga Salt Springs in forty years' working. The product the first year was 4,000 barrels, and over 600,000 the last, making in all 5,626,326 barrels of salt in ten years. Adding up the lumber table makes the nice sum of 2,930,493,075 feet.

The transportation of lumber brings into service nearly one hundred barges, with a capacity of about 25,000,000 feet. Ship building is becoming an important branch of industry.

AUXILIARY RESOURCES.

Lumber and salt are not the only resources of the city and Valley. At Alabaster, on the shore, and embraced within the Valley trade, are the plaster beds, yielding about 40,000 tons of plaster annually, of the best quality. To the south lie the newly discovered coal beds. These are located in Shiawassee, just south of Saginaw county. On the west is the celebrated

ST. LOUIS MAGNETIC WELL,

thirty miles from Saginaw, and connected by an excellent plank road. I should have said magnetic wells, for there is any number of them at St. Louis, as, in fact, all over the

State of Michigan. By boring from two to fifteen hundred feet, an almost impenetrable strata of rock is reached, after which the auger will sometimes drop fifteen or eighteen inches, and water, strongly charged with electricity, gushes to the top, rising often as high as twenty-five feet above the surface of the earth. Of course when the water is exposed to the air, it soon loses its magnetic properties, which makes it necessary for a patient to dwell in the close vicinity of a well, in order to derive any benefit.

The St. Louis magnetic spring, as it is called, (it is a well) was discovered in 1869, when boring for salt. Prof. Duffield was immediately called upon to make an analysis, which he did, as below, calculated on the imperial gallon. Temperature of water, 50 deg. constant. Specific gravity, 1,011:

	Grains.
Sulphate Lime	66.50
Silicate Lime	6.72
Chloride, a trace.	
Bi-Carbonate Soda	106.40
" Lime	69.40
" Magnesia	17.50
" Iron	1.20
Silica free	2.88
Organic matter and loss	2.00
Total constituents	272.60
Bi-Carbonates	194-62
Free Carbonic Acid in Gallon	6.21
Sulphureted Hydrogen, traces.	
Total Mineral Matter in a Gallon	279.60

The Professor is slow to dilate upon its curative properties, but salutary or not, they have become exceedingly popular— the springs bidding fair to rival Saratoga as a watering place.

There can be no mistake, however, about their curative properties. Too many invalids have been benefited thereby. I have seen several since my return. Among others, a young and talented editor, of Northern Indiana, who was entirely cured of paralysis by a short sojourn at these famous wells.

For the following graphic and valuable notice of the St. Louis Magnetic Springs, I am indebted to Mr. Turner, of the Louisville *Industrial and Commercial Gazette.* He and his family spent several days there after our return from the Saginaw Valley:

"The most direct route to these newly famed springs, is via Saginaw City, from which a fine plank road extends the whole distance of thirty miles, through wild, romantic scenery, giving the tourist a few glimpses of life in the back-woods on a small scale. Large, roomy stages of the 'Concord' pattern make daily trips to and fro. Wayside inns occur every few miles, and neat little cottages occasionally peer out from their shady inclosures. The time occupied in making the trip is from four and a half to five hours, and the ride being principally through the forest, shady and cool. Surmounting a gentle slope, the pretty village of St. Louis lies spread out in the quiet valley before us—a sweet, rural picture, with its frame of wood-covered slopes. The fresh, white cottages, the larger hotel buildings, the church spires, and the bright-colored flag on the right denotes the where-abouts of the famous Wah-wah-sum Springs. A moment more and the stage reaches the Eastman House, recently built by William H. Taylor, Esq., its genial host. The table is first-class, and the rooms much larger and better furnished than is usual at places of summer resort. A verandah extends around two sides of the building, with a broad balcony leading from the second story in front. There are several other hotels, and those who desire excellent private boarding, can procure good quarters at very reasonable rates, varying from four to seven dollars per week. It is about five minutes' walk to the bath house of the Magnetic Springs, a building said to be the largest and best in America. The center building, containing the reception and waiting rooms, is two stories high, surmounted by a tasteful cupola. On either side are long one-story wings, containing the baths, one side arranged for the females, the other for the male sex.

"In the rear runs Pine river; in front extends a lawn of several acres, with plank walks reaching in various directions. Young shade trees have been set out, and add much to the inviting appearance of the grounds. Crossing a little foot bridge, we come to the spring-house, a tower-shaped structure, such as is seen in the oil regions. In the center is the iron tubing, from which issues, in inexhaustable supply, the water of crystal pureness, which has been the means of such wonderful cures. Below is an iron supply pipe, four inches in diameter, which extends to the bath-house.

"We should mention that the entire length of this house is one hundred and eighty feet, containing twenty baths in each wing.

"Pine river, a tributary of the Saginaw, nearly encircles the town, and furnishes water power sufficient to operate a large saw-mill adjoining the spring. The scenery along its banks is very attractive, and its waters contain an abundance of fine fish. The site of St. Louis is one hundred and fifty feet above Saginaw City, and the atmosphere is cool and salubrious. A trip to this point well repays the visitor, while the necessary expenses are scarcely one-half of those of the more fashionable springs. To persons contemplating a visit, we would advise the following route: From Louis-ville via Jeffersonville, Madison and Indianapolis R. R.; thence over the Bee Line and Muncie route, connecting with the Fort Wayne and Muncie Railroad to Fort Wayne, stopping over night; via Fort Wayne and Jackson, and Jackson, Lansing and Saginaw railroads to Saginaw City; stop over night, or longer, at the Taylor House; thence by stage to the destination."

THE SAGINAW LIMESTONE,

as shown by careful analysis, is of the very best quality. The quarries are located on Stone Island, which lies on the east side of Saginaw Bay, about twenty-four miles from the Saginaw river. The marl deposits are also rich and extensive. During 1869, an extensive marl bed was develope don the Saginaw river, north side, midway between East Saginaw and Bay City. The marl is pronounced to be a fertilizer almost equal to guano.

AGRICULTURE.

The city is surrounded by a very rich and productive region, one that in quality is fully equal to, and in extent far surpasses, the far-famed Genesee Valley of Western New York. As yet the agricultural resources are, to a large extent, undeveloped, but owing to the brisk demand and high prices for farm products, caused by the manufacturing industry, more attention is being given in that direction, and it proves largely remunerative.

RAILROAD FACILITIES.

The Flint and Pere Marquette Railroad, connected at Holly with the Detroit and Milwaukie, is the pioneer, and will be be completed to Lake Michigan in 1872.

The Bay City and East Saginaw Railroad is operated by the Flint and Pere Marquette Railroad Company.

The Jackson, Lansing and Saginaw Railroad.

ROADS UNDER CONTRACT.

To St. Louis magnetic springs, connecting with the Grand Rapids and Chicago; to St. Clair, on the St. Clair River, to form a part of the Chicago Southern Railway, and from East Saginaw to Ann Arbor.

The county of Saginaw is sixth in population in the State, (39,095,) and twelfth in valuation.

CHAPTER XIV.

FAREWELL TO THE VALLEY.

At Saginaw we were honored with a dispatch from Mr. D. McLaren, General Superintendent of the Cincinnati, Hamilton and Dayton Railroad, tendering the hospitalities of that road to Lima, and similar invitations were extended by C. E. Gorham, Superintendent of the Pittsburg, Fort Wayne and Chicago Railroad, and by Doctor Potter, President of the Flint and Pere Marquette Railroad. Upon account of special arrangements for our return home, we were obliged to decline these much esteemed courtesies.

THE PARTING.

When the time, "it came to part" from our Saginaw Valley friends, in the regret experienced, we were made to feel the hold they had taken on our affection and respect. In the language of the *Enterprise* that morning:

> "The bridegroom may forget the bride
> 'Twas made his wedded wife yestreen,
> The monarch may forget the crown
> That on his head an hour has been,
> The mother may forget the child
> That smiles sae sweetly on her knee,
> But we'll remember you, our friends,
> And the pleasures we have shared with thee."

At half past 8 Friday morning, there was a general meeting of the excursionists at Saginaw city, which was well attended by the citizens of the Valley. The utmost social enthusiasm prevailed. A committee of the excursionists submitted the following resolutions which were received and adopted with genuine applause:

The excursion party from Tennessee, Kentucky, Indiana, Ohio and other States, on the eve of their departure from the Saginaw Valley for their respective homes, beg leave to offer the following resolutions:

Resolved, That the excursion under the superintendence of Mr. Grafton has been a grand success.

Resolved, That to the people of East Saginaw City and Bay City, we return our heartfelt thanks for a generous hospitality, evidenced by unnumbered kindnesses extended with open hearts.

Resolved, That we can not leave the Saginaw Valley without expressing our sense of appreciation of their industry, their skill and tact, and that we have no hesitancy in pronouncing their labors unexampled in the history of the Union, everywhere considered the synonym of progress and enterprise.

Resolved, That in taking our leave and saying farewell, we do so with a regret as deep' as the admiration for the people of Saginaw Valley is high.

R. LOWRY,
J. M. KEATING.
W. B. VICKERS.

At a meeting of the Cincinnati delegation, held the evening before, at the Bancroft House, East Saginaw, June 8, 1871, the following resolutions were framed and heartily approved:

"*Resolved*, That the delegation of citizens of Cincinnati beg leave to express their thanks to the following persons for kindness and courtesies extended to them during the excursion trip to Saginaw bay: Mr. J. H. Sheldon, Superintendent Cincinnati and Indianapolis Junction Railroad; Mr. W. W. Worthington, Superintendent Fort Wayne, Muncie and Cincinnati Railroad; Mr. William A. Ernst, Superintendent Fort Wayne, Jackson and Saginaw Railroad; Mr. A. Watson, Superintendent Jackson, Lansing and Saginaw Railroad; and to all the other officers and employes of these roads, and to the committee of arrangements, and to the citizens of Fort Wayne, Jackson, Saginaw city, East Saginaw and Bay City, for their hospitable attentions and whole-souled liberality shown us during our visit and stay among them. We have found the spirit of enterprise and growth of these cities far beyond anything we had expected, and we are satisfied that these new lines of communication with our city will add an element of material progress that will be of great advantage to the trade and commerce of our people, and we have no doubt that the acquaintance so pleasantly begun will be continued to our mutual advantage in the future. We also tender our thanks to Dr. H. C. Potter, Superintendent and Treasurer of the Flint and Pere Marquette Railroad, for an invitation to pass over his road, which we find impossible to accept at this time."

LEWIS WORTHINGTON,
T. R. BIGGS,
MILES GREENWOOD,
DR. C. G. COMEGYS,
L. H. SARGENT,
GAZZAM GANO.
JAMES L. HAVEN,
JOSEPH KINSEY,
H. L. LAWS,
OLIVER KINSEY,
L. S. WORTHINGTON.
A. L. ANDREWS,

MRS. L. WORTHINGTON,
MRS. MILES GREENWOOD,
MRS. T. R. BIGGS,
MRS. J. H. LAWS,
MRS. J. L. HAVEN,
MRS. A. L. ANDREWS,
MRS. G. GANO,
MISS SALLIE MEAD,
MISS MAGGIE BONNER,
MISS HATTIE GANO.

The general meeting was held at the depot and broke up with three cheers and a tiger, which we could hear above the whistle of the locomotive as we steamed up the valley.

CHAPTER XV.

HOMEWARD BOUND.

Once more *en route*, we were not forsaken by our new friends. They accompanied us to the return station where we were met by our Jackson friends. Their kind faces were very welcome. The trip to Jackson was occupied in lively conversation, all of us feeling, by this time, perfectly at home with each other.

THE MICHIGAN STATE PRISON.

The train halted the other side of Jackson to allow us an opportunity of visiting the State Prison. Here we were received by Mr. John Morris, the agent or warden, (as we call the official), who conducted us to the prison. It was high noon, and we had an opportunity of seeing the prisoners march in to dinner. There were six or seven hundred of them, and as, with their striped uniform on, they filed along the irregular stone walls in locks of fifty, they bore more of a resemblance to the fabled sea serpent than to human beings. They were very human, as their appreciation of a few feeble words of sympathy abundantly proved. All unused to public speaking, it was in my heart to say much that was kind and profitable, but the words fell cold and weak from my lips. Had I been accustomed to a sea of faces, I should have been overwhelmed by the spectacle of nearly a thousand men in bonds. With their eager, sorrowful eyes fixed upon me, I can not describe the feeling of relief when the silence was broken by a shout, as I said, I hoped to meet them again on the other side of the prison walls. I meant to assure them that there was plenty of room in the busy world outside for them—that the world stands in need of just such good citizens as they, with their habits of industry, order and obedience, can become.

In a conversation with Mr. John Morris, the agent of the prison, he said:

"In this shop" (we were passing through a spoke and lath shop), "there has not been a discredit mark for sixty days."

"You then commute sentence with good behavior?"

"Yes, that is our custom, and it works well. You would be surprised at the time some of the prisoners gain. They are not, after all, such a bad set of men. I took charge of them, I confess, with some degree of nervousness, but, with kind treatment, they are a quiet, well ordered people.

"I find there is policy and profit, as well as humanity, in kind treatment. My experience, thus far, sustains me fully, in abating much of the severity formerly deemed indispensible in such institutions. The greatest problem with me is, who shall help me in the management of those men I want men of kind, humane dispositions, but always even and firm in discipline—men whose strength lies in heart, not in muscle."

Mr. Morris dwelt at some length on his duty to fit these prisoners for a responsible place in the world, when the term of their imprisonment shall have expired; and gave me many interesting instances of reform, which I have not space to include in this writing. He gave me, also, the workings of the abolition of capital punishment—statistics to prove its salutary effect, sustained by examples of pardon extended to life convicts. The system of solitary confinement at hard labor is virtually abolished. It was impracticable, as far as labor went, and had a cruel effect upon the prisoner. After a short time, he almost invariably became insane. At the time of our visit there was but one of the prisoners confined in his cell. He was detected making his escape, and is, in nature, more nearly allied to the brute than to human creation.

There were only seven female convicts—one for the diversion of killing her father-in-law, a colored woman for murdering three little step-children. The prison itself seemed to be in splendid condition—clean, well ventilated, and freshly whitewashed. The prison fare is wholesome and abundant.

MR. WEBSTER AGAIN.

An important industry connected with the prison, is the wagon manufactory of Austin, Tomlinson & Webster. They employ two hundred convicts, and a large number of free men. They occupy a building 50x400 feet, two stories high, with a 30 feet ell for an engine room. Ten acres of land and a dozen store houses are used for the wagons, as they are turned out of the shops, and for storing material, etc. The engine is eighty horse-power, and the best of machinery is used in every department of the work.

My readers will remember the fine army wagons, which, a little while ago, were common on the streets. The most substantial of them were manufactured by this company. It is said, also, that these wagons are the only ones that will stand the wear and tear of a trip to California. Others, less highly seasoned and carefully built, fall to pieces with the heat of the plains. Last year this company manufactured between six and seven thousand wagons.

SEEING US HOME.

Once more aboad, the Fort Wayne, Jackson and Saginaw Railroad Company renewed our obligations, by serving us, with their own hands, a bountiful repast. That is, those of them who, as the children say, came a piece of the way home with us. Need I add that we parted from them with unfeigned regret.

Mayor Randall had arranged that we should again be the guests of Fort Wayne, and we spent the night in that delightful city. But there was a gloom over it which the offices of hospitality could not dispel. Two nights before there had been a terrific explosion of rose oil, by which several citizens were killed and wounded, and considerable property destroyed. In face of these facts, a vender of rose oil comes out in a card and says: "It is the safest, cleanest and best illuminating oil in use."

CONCLUSION.

Bidding our Fort Wayne friends adieu, Saturday morning we took our last departure homeward. Now, partings began to multiply on us, our fellow travelers dropping off, one by one, or in parties, at the different stations. The Benhams, Turners and Jacobs, we had left at Saginaw, for a fishing *bout*, and we, in turn, were left behind by our Southern friends. I am sure all will join me in saying, it was a most enjoyable trip, undisturbed by any infelicities, or the shadow of discontent.

TESTIMONIALS.

CINCINNATI TESTIMONIAL.

The Saginaw Valley Excursion— What the Excursionists Saw— Importance of the New Railroad Connections to Cincinnati— Thanks.

CINCINNATI, June 10, 1871.

To the Cincinnati Board of Trade and Chamber of Commerce:

Your committee appointed to go with an excursion to celebrate the opening of the line of road, making a new, all rail, unbroken connection for Cincinnati, of over three hundred and sixty miles, with the Saginaw Valley and Lake Huron, making an era in the history of our city that needs only to be improved to be of vast importance to us, beg leave to report that we left Cincinnati, via the Cincinnati, Hamilton and Dayton Railroad, on the 6th inst., at 7:06 o'clock. Arriving at Hamilton, we took the Indianapolis and Cincinnati Junction Railroad for Connersville, on our way stopping at the following places:

CITY.	Miles from Cincinnati.	Population.
Connersville, Ind	50	3,500
Cambridge City, Ind	80	2,500
Newcastle, Ind	85	2,500
Muncie, Ind	105	3,500
Fort Wayne, Ind	175	20,000
Jackson, Michigan	275	14,000
Saginaw City, Mich	376	8,000
East Saginaw, Mich	378	13,000
Winona, Mich	391	2,000
Portsmouth, Mich	391	2,000
Bay City, Mich	393	8,000
Bangor, Mich	303	2,000

While our city has been struggling and making vain efforts to get a direct railroad connection south, our interests toward the north have been in a measure overlooked; but, in the meantime, the links in this northern line of roads have been quietly united, that bring within easy reach of our enterprise the commerce of two large States, already teeming with a live and enterprising population, producing the raw materials that our manufacturing industry consumes, at lowest cost, and consuming the products of our manufactures, and ready to share our commerce on terms that we can offer in competition with any market within their reach.

At Fort Wayne, Indiana, we found them making machinery and wagon work on a very large scale, and consuming some of the manufactures of iron brought from Connecticut that are made and sold in our market of better quality and at cheaper prices than are to be found elsewhere. This, in connection with the fact that we can now—thanks to the Fort Wayne, Muncie and Cincinnati Railroad—offer them low rates of freight, should induce a large portion of their valuable trade to come back to us, that has been diverted to other places. At the city of Jackson, Michigan, energy, thrift and enterprise were apparent on every hand, and your committee, one and all, expressed the greatest surprise to see the growth and magnitude of this young city. On reaching Saginaw, we found within a radius of a few miles on an arm of lake Huron, a population of fifty thousand people—all thriving and prosperous, with street railroads, well paved streets and commodious first-class hotels—making up a community that can only be appreciated by seeing them. Our delegation was received everywhere with the utmost cordiality, and every pains taken to show us the results of their industry. We saw mills that had a capacity of forty million feet per annum. Salt works which from a production of four thousand barrels in 1860 reached a production of 645,516 barrels in 1870. This vast industry necessarily consumes a large amount of material in the way of machinery, oils, soap, candles, belting, tools, etc., and our manufacturers and merchants should take pains to canvass this trade, which may in time be made vastly profitable to both sections of the country. We are the natural distributing point for the sugar and molasses of Louisiana, and the cotton fabrics manufactured in the south, who already have their agents established here. For this important connection with this rich section of country we are indebted to our enterprising fellow citizen, Lewis Worthington, and his associates, who have made this for Cincinnati at great personal sacrifice, yet it must stand an enduring monument to their character as liberal citizens and men of enterprise.

The Cincinnati delegation held a meeting last Thursday evening, the 8th inst., to return their thanks for the many favors shown them during their stay, a copy of which we herewith inclose in our report. We think the people of that section of the country should be invited to visit our city at an early day.　　Respectfully,

Gazzam Gano,

J. L. Haven,

Miles Greenwood,

Committee from Board of Trade.

T. R. Biggs,

L. H. Sargent,

H. L. Laws,

Committee from Chamber of Commerce.

TESTIMONIALS OF THE PRESS.

The recent completion of the Muncie route to the great lumber and salt regions of the Saginaw Valley is of immense importance to our State and the South, it forming the connecting link of an almost air line between the two sections, and placing our dealers in easy and direct communication with the producer, thereby enabling us to compete with any market. By means of the new connection lumber can be loaded on cars at Saginaw and landed in Louisville in three days, without re-handling. By the old routes, via Chicago or Detroit, it required from nine to thirteen days. The condition of the track throughout is superior to most roads, and the rolling stock is new and handsomely constructed. The lumber is placed directly from the mills upon the Jackson,

Lansing and Saginaw Railroad, thence over the Jackson and Fort Wayne road, connecting with the Fort Wayne and Muncie Railroad to Indianapolis, forming an unbroken line of rail for freight. This opportunity should be taken advantage of at once by Louisville dealers.—*J. H. Turner, Industrial and Commercial Gazette, Louisville, Kentucky.*

Next morning, at half-past eight o'clock, we started on our return trip, but before leaving the Saginaw Valley, we must not fail to acknowledge the spontaneous hospitality of her people, respect their enterprise, envy their prosperity, and turn upon the *Enterprise* with the same quotation which it used in bidding us good by:

> " The bridegroom may forget the bride
> 'Twas made his wedded wife yestreen,
> The monarch may forget the crown
> That on his head an hour hath been,
> The mother may forget the child
> That smiles sae sweetly on her knee,
> But we'll remember you, our friends,
> And the pleasures we have shared with you."

—*E. R. Zeller, Oxford (Ohio) Citizen.*

The public buildings, the hotels, and the large dwellings in these "sister cities" are built in the most modern styles and designs. Everything has the appearance of enterprise and prosperity. In no other city in the land have they such saw mills, such salt works, such whole-souled people, such live business men, and such—shall we say it?—pretty women as are found here.—*R. H. Weamer, Steuben Republican.*

EXCURSION TO THE BIG WOODS.—We went up in Michigan last week with a lot of editors and civilians, on a voyage of discovery. We started expecting to surprise somebody. We come back feeling that somebody up north had surprised us. We took our wives along, expecting, at least, to make the Indians and other natives stare. We came back with a kind of vague idea that we had seen the country that wives first came from, (though, of course, we felt we had the best of them.) We went expecting to eat up everything they had, and then intended to call for more, but the more we ate and drank the more there seemed to be left. It is difficult to describe our trip. The more we think about it the less we want to say, for nothing but wild adjectives can do it justice, and they all seem tame when harnessed in here. Imagine a company of a hundred and fifty ladies and gentlemen, with a pre-determination to like each other, with a train of palace coaches placed at their disposal for a run through a most interesting country, new to almost the entire party, and the people along the line vieing with each other in kindness and whole-souled hospitality to their guests, people which may justly be called the first of all this great Yankee nation in intelligence, enterprise and thrift, and you have some idea of what the Saginaw excursionists had to suffer. As before stated, the whole trip is summed up by saying, we started out to capture, and got captured ourselves.—*A. C. Melette, Muncie Times.*

The stranger, in Jackson, and in these valley cities, can not fail to be impressed with the magnificence of the public and private buildings, and the progressive spirit exhibited in all those features of a town which indicate taste, intelligence, and an appreciation of art. While, by active industry, they readily acquire wealth, they seem to appreciate that wealth only as it may be used in beautifying their homes, in developing a higher condition of intelligence, and in drawing others to them by a lavish and cordial hospitality and the utmost good fellowship.—*George S. Brown, Correspondent Indiana Herald, Huntington, Indiana.*

We regret, very much, that the crowded state of our columns will not permit an extended mention of the many attentions and whole-souled liberality extended by the citizens of Fort Wayne, Jackson, Saginaw City, East Saginaw, and Bay City. We also regret that we are unable to give a proper description of the excellent country through which these roads pass, and the immense resources which account for the wealth and advancement of a country which, but a few years ago, was an unbroken wilderness.

The heartfelt thanks of the entire party are due Messrs. Worthington, Grafton, and others, who did everything that could add, in the least, to the comfort and happiness of the excursionsists.—*J. Craig, Blufton Banner.*

GREAT RESOURCES OF THE SAGINAW VALLEY.

It shall now be our object to give to those of your readers who were unable to accompany the party a more full and complete history of the trip, the enjoyments and other items of interest connected with the same, but above all shall we endeavor to convey to the mind of the reader some definite idea of the great resources of the Saginaw Valley and its tributaries, the untold amount of wealth contained therein, the enterprise and public spirit everywhere recognized among its inhabitants, and should we thereby be the means of encouraging a commercial, as well as a social intercourse between the citizens of the great valley of the Saginaw and those of the Mississippi valley and Southern States, we feel that an object will be achieved that will redound not only to the pecuniary advantage of both sections, but to the lasting perpetuity of a friendly intercourse that is but in its pristine state at this period.—*F. S. Shurich, Agent Associated Press, Correspondent Cincinnati Gazette.*

THE WONDERFUL VALLEY OF THE SAGINAW.

We have a task before us which is both pleasant and painful; to write of our visit to the wonderful valley of the Saginaw. It is pleasant to write, because the time we spent in going, coming and while we were there, was the most pleasant of our life; it is painful because we are conscious of our inability to do the subject justice.

By the completion and opening of the Fort Wayne, Muncie and Cincinnati Railroad—of recent occurrence—a new line of commerce has been inaugurated. The heart of the great pine region of the north has been pierced, and the lumber trade, heretofore running around by Toledo, Cleveland and Buffalo, is set directly South, so that we get lumber and salt direct, instead of by the circuitous route heretofore employed.—*John O. Hardesty, Anderson Herald.*

COUNTRY OF VAST RESOURCES AND ENERGETIC PEOPLE.

The limited time which the party were permitted to remain in the Valley, precluded the possibility of seeing all worth seeing—a month could be profitably spent there—but they remained long enough there to discover that it is a country of vast resources, both in an agricultural and manufacturing point of view; that the people are energetic and wide-awake as to their business interests; and, while attending to those, they do not forget the educational part, as is shown by the magnificent school buildings in some of the cities—the one in Saginaw City would be a credit to any city in the country.— *E. H. Bundy, Democratic Times, Muncie, Ind.*

EXTRAORDINARY GROWTH OF THE NORTH-WEST.

The people of the Northwest, not satisfied with the wonderful growth of agricultural products, have copied the example of England; have found in the profound depths of a soil which yields most abundantly, a mineral wealth which, by the aid of brawny arms and stout hearts, they skillfully fashion into machines of extraordinary capacity, increasing facilities for manufactures that find a demand as needy as their power to satisfy. The Northwest, with a constantly increasing population demanding aids and assistants in the work of developing the country, was forced to have recourse to mechanical devices and machines, while the South, stimulated by a world's demand for cotton, enlarged her area of growth for that staple and saved from his vices the negro machine, not more reliable or intelligent than those, which, guided by the northwestern farmer and manufacturer, have built towns and cities, and made a garden out of a wilderness. And not only this, the means of education and personal culture have kept pace with the work of material development, evidenced in magnificent school houses maintained at the public expense, and other institutions of a practical and beneficent character. From the hour I left.—*J. M. Keating, Memphis Appeal.*

A MOST ENERGETIC AND HOSPITABLE PEOPLE.

Hire we are safe in Memphis, after an absence of eight days, during which we traveled some thousands of miles, and met with many incidents not only pleasant to remember but probably of interest to many Southern tourists who may be ready to take their annual departure for cooler and healthier climes. Heretofore the Southern people have thought that a trip to that attractive and progressive part of the world known as North Michigan, lying on the shores of Lake Huron, necessarily involved a circuitous pilgrimage by way of Chicago, or the more Eastern and tortuous route by way of Sandusky, Toledo and Detroit. But this idea has been put to flight by the opening of a central railroad through route connecting Louisville and Cincinnati directly with the city of Saginaw, which outrivals "Duluth," and is one of the most enterprising as well as hospitable places in the country. This region has had no direct connection with the Ohio river, and was supposed by the refined people of the outside world to be inhabited by a race of wood-choppers, hunters and salt-boilers, who afforded a fine opening for missionary efforts. How we have to change our opinions often, and feel like asking others to do the same, may be inferred from the pleasant surprise enjoyed on this trip, at finding ourselves, as Southern men, welcomed with unstinted liberality by communities of highly educated, refined and prosperous people; and how we made not only acquaintances but friends worthy to be claimed and remembered as such with pride and pleasure, are matters which none can doubt who read this feeble description of our reception and entertainment.—*E. Whitmore, Public Ledger, Memphis.*

A JOYOUS OCCASION.

Of the excursion, we may say this: That it was gotten up by those who had the management of the undertaking, without sparing anything that could render it either pleasant or profitable to the guests. The citizens of Fort Wayne, Jackson and Saginaw, opened their hearts in displaying their generous hospitality, in a manner that the editors will never forget. The company, as may well be imagined, enjoyed themselves as only men who are hard worked and closely confined during the greater part of their lives, can enjoy themselves. It was emphatically a joyous occasion. It was more than this. It was the uniting and commingling of representations of the press from sections of the country, but a short time ago bitterly hostile to each other. It was an opportunity for them to discover, not how many causes of difference existed between them, but how many points of agreement there were. It was a time for men and women to find how much nearer they were to each other than they had supposed, how much better and kinder they found out their friends to be than they had imagined.

Much is due to Messrs. Worthington and Grafton, for the fine manner in which everything was conducted.—*Samuel Davenport, Bluffton Chronicle.*

GROWTH AND WEALTH OF SAGINAW.

"In the limited space allowed for a single letter I can not say anything, in what room is left for this one, of the wonderful growth and accumulated wealth of Saginaw. The telegraph has advised you of the princely manner in which our party was received and entertained at the different stopping places. If General Grant and all the members of his cabinet had been with us, we would not and could not have been treated with more consideration and entertained in a more hospitable and sumptuous manner. We were feasted and toasted at every convenient opportunity. Private houses were thrown open, hotels were at our disposal, "without money and without price," and carriages were subject to order whenever wanted for visiting any point of interest. The entire period has been one of unbounded and unmarred pleasure never to be forgotten by those who participated in the scenes of joy that have surrounded us."—*R. W. Weamer, Steuben Republican.*

GREAT SAGINAW ROUTE TO THE PACIFIC.

This excursion was in the interest of the new roads leading from Cincinnati and the South through Muncie, Fort Wayne, Jackson and Lansing to Saginaw, thence soon to Mackinaw, to connect with roads from Duluth and the Northern Pacific. Members of the press, railroad men and others, with their ladies, were invited from all along the line and off the line, and though it was an unmitigatedly inexpensive journey to the invited guests, no expense or pains were spared by the railroads or the citizens of any of the towns through which we passed, and it seemed entirely divested of any advertising air, sometimes given to excursions. Everybody showed us their possessions and advantages, because they were proud of them, and glad to have the chance to divide a little with appreciative neighbors. The wealth and enterprise of the country through which we passed deserves to be known.— *B. Moffatt, Springfield Republican, Ohio.*

THE GROWTH OF TEN YEARS.

We presume it is hardly necessary to add that the excursionists were very agreeably surprised to find a large city here instead of a small backwoods town as they expected. We find here a city of ten or twelve thousand inhabitants, filled with magnificent buildings and palatial residences. The railroad connections and steamboat navigation of the Saginaw river, the bay and the lakes, has, in the short space of ten years, converted the dense wilderness into a large and beautiful city. The lumbermen are no longer lumbermen camping in the wilderness of the pineries, but capitalists and wholesale dealers in this prosperous city.—*J. S. Jennings, Marion, Ind., Mississinewa Monitor.*

ENERGY AND ENTERPRISE OF MICHIGAN.

The invitation was extended to us by the Fort Wayne, Muncie and Cincinnati Railroad Company, a company that has completed a very important link in the chain of roads, binding the vast pine forests, saw mills and salt works of Michigan to Southern Indiana and Ohio.

It was the first time we had had the pleasure of seeing that section of country, and on every hand we were equally surprised and delighted with the spirit of energy and enterprise that has built up the handsome towns and cities, which dotted our route, the spirit which is manifested in Michigan, in the tillage of their fertile fields, and in the clearing of thousands of acres of magnificent forest growth, which has crowded the banks on both sides of the Saginaw river for twenty miles with large piles of lumber and with innumerable saw logs, and which has drilled many artesian wells for salt water, and has manufactured from the brine immense quantities of beautiful crystalized salt.—*A. Converse, Christian Observer, Louisville.*

WHAT THE SAGINAW VALLEY IS LIKE.

The Saginaw Valley more nearly resembles a vast bee-hive than any place I have ever seen. Full fifteen miles of broad river is lined on either bank with immense mills and "salt blocks," and thousands of men are driving ahead by steam, day and night, turning out lumber in every shape, which is shipped to the four quarters of the habitable globe. Some of these mills are so immense that no mere description of them can be credited, and the aggregate of the business done here is so tremendous that it must be seen to be believed.

My thanks are due to so many corporations and individuals, for various favors cheerfully rendered, that I can only thank them collectively and hope that we may meet again in 1872.—*W. B. Vickers, Saturday Evening Mirror, Indianapolis.*

NATURAL OUTLET OF THE PENINSULAR STATE.

SAGINAW.—The river bearing that name, and on the banks of which the city of Saginaw, East Saginaw and Bay City, with intermediate towns of lesser note are situated, is the natural outlet for the vast lumber region of the Peninsular State. Here we found within a radius of a few miles on an arm of Lake Huron, a population of 50,000 people—all thriving and prosperous, with street railroads, well-paved streets, and commodious first-class hotels—making up a community that can only be appreciated by seeing them.—*Howard Briggs, Indiana Press, Greencastle, Ind.*

HUNTING THE BAY AND THE WILDERNESS.

In the morning a drive around Saginaw, East Saginaw and South Saginaw was the first order, and in company with Mr. Braley, ex-Mayor of Saginaw, and behind a three minute pony, I made the circuit. Of course the first thing I asked for was the bay. Imagine my astonishment and pity my geography, when I learned that Saginaw City was on Saginaw river, some sixteen miles from Saginaw Bay. The next time I make a journey, a study of the map shall be my first thought. The drive showed that instead of there being only a lumber station somewhere in the wilds of a Michigan forest, there were three towns so closely connected as to be in reality one, and having fine stores, elegant dwellings, brick business blocks, hotels that put to shame those in Indianapolis, as mine host, Wesley of the Bates, can testify, Nicolson pavements, and twenty-five thousand people.—*A. J. Halford, Journal, Indianapolis.*

HEAD CENTER OF CIVILIZATION.

The next morning we took carriages again, and from their cushions inspected Saginaw City, East Saginaw and South Saginaw. Saw mills, salt blocks, shingle shops, log rafts, lath factories, palatial stores, residences with swell fronts, south exposure, and Nicolson pavements flitted by us and circled round us to our infinite amazement. We were looking for Indians, wigwams, squaws, pappooses, bows and arrows, bears and red leggins, but if they ever were here they had vanished, and cities of splendor had arisen in the wilderness.— *A. M. Benham, Musical Review, Indianapolis.*

THRIFT AND WEALTH OF THE SAGINAW VALLEY.

To say that the excursionists from Indiana and the South were astonished at the appearance of thrift and wealth in the

Saginaw Valley, is to speak in very measured terms. Just imagine twenty-seven miles of river front, the shore on either side lined with rafts of pine logs, continuous piles of lumber in the back ground, and back of these, saw mills and salt works thickly sandwiched.

Such is the rapidity with which the rough log is cut into lumber, that a boat may land at the wharf with an order, and the lumber will be sawed and placed on board as rapidly as it can be loaded from the dock.

We should be pleased to say more of this wonderful country and generous, hospitable people.—*P. S. Westfall, Manager Terre Haute Express.*

CAPITAL FISHING AT SAGINAW BAY.

Tarrying behind the great majority of the excursionists, we enjoyed for a few days longer, than they, the generous hospitality of the people of Saginaw City. For several days we had seemingly been looking upon a panorama of brilliant sights, which was unrolled at railroad speed from the capital of Indiana to the head waters of Saginaw Bay; and we were not loth to give heed to the urgent invitation of our new friends to stay a little longer, and "go a fishing." Our host Hopkins, of the Taylor House, Saginaw City, with his efficient lieutenant, Armstrong, "seconded the motion," and so we allowed trunks to rest on their castors while we prepared our lighter traps for handy use on the river.

This new northern route is destined to be a favorite one with the traveling public.

The cities of the valley, Saginaw, East Saginaw and Bay City, are all flourishing and prosperous towns, and have excellent hotels. We thoroughly tested and enjoyed the hospitalities of all of them.—*Charles P. Jacobs, Evening News.*

THE KIND, GENEROUS AND INDOMITABLE MICHIGANDERS.

To see now, in the midst of a surrounding wilderness, where, in 1850, were only two or three log houses, two lively cities of nine and eleven thousand inhabitants, with their hotels, rivaling in beauty and merit those of Chicago, with their elegant private residences, with their beautiful business houses, their street railways, and their eighty thousand dollar school houses, was enough to fill the minds of the visitors with combined surprise and admiration at the wonderful energy and enterprise of the indomitable Michiganders. This surprise and admiration continued to increase during our entire sojourn of two nights and a day in this never to be forgotten Valley of the Saginaw. But time calls us to tell of all the kindness, generosity and public spirit of these chivalrous Michiganders. Let them be assured that it touched and won the hearts of all. Nor shall we soon forget our obligations to the courtesy and far-sightedness of the officers of the roads over which we traveled, to all members of the party, whose pleasant companionship we enjoyed, is herewith extended cordial and fraternal greeting. They will doubtless be glad to join in the following chorus:

> Long live the Michiganders,
> John Grafton, long live he,
> And when he next doth rise abroad,
> May we be there to see.

—*Robert McNeice, Editor Gazette, Fort Wayne.*

THE LARGEST SAW MILLS IN THE WORLD.

The saw mills, on the Saginaw river, are said to be the largest and most efficient in the world—at any rate, we know that it takes less time for one of the gang-saws to rip a log into lumber than it does to tell about it. Now, that these roads to the South are open, and under such excellent management, regions which have been dependent on Chicago, should look to this section for their supply of lumber. As far as the eye can reach, vast quantities of lumber are to be seen waiting transportation to those parts of the country where it is needed.—*Col. S. Merrill, Muncie Telegraph.*

$20,000,000 A YEAR.

THE SAGINAW VALLEY.—Cincinnati, thanks mainly to private enterprise, is now in direct railway connection with the Saginaw Valley of Michigan. There was lately an excursion into that country, in which several of our citizens participated, and in another place we print, from a correspondent, a full description of that wonderfully productive region. This is worthy of the attention of our merchants and manufacturers, who should begin to look into the resources and study the wants of that section, with a view to making use of the one and supplying the other.

A valley that produces, in one year, lumber, shingles, staves, salt, plaster, etc., to the value of $20,000,000, and is rapidly increasing, is a valley that Cincinnati people should know all about.—*Cincinnati Gazette.*

THE GREAT SAGINAW ROUTE.

WHITE WATER VALLEY RAILROAD

CONNECTS WITH

FORT WAYNE, MUNCIE & CINCINNATI R. R.,

FORMING THE

FIRST SOUTHERN SECTION

IN THE

THE GREAT SAGINAW ROUTE.

H. M. BRITTON, Superintendent, Cincinnati.

Fort Wayne, Muncie & Cincinnati R. R.

NEW AND POPULAR SHORT ROUTE

FROM INDIANAPOLIS TO FORT WAYNE,

JACKSON, SAGINAW, GRAND RAPIDS, KALAMAZOO, TOLEDO, MONROE, DETROIT,

AND ALL POINTS IN MICHIGAN and CANADA,

VIA MUNCIE.

Be Sure and Ask for Tickets at the Union Depot via Muncie.

FARE AS LOW AND TIME AS QUICK AS ANY OTHER ROUTE.

CONNECTIONS SURE.

JOHN J. GRAFTON,
Pass. Ag't.

W. W. WORTHINGTON,
Supt. and Gen'l Ag't.

FORT WAYNE, JACKSON AND SAGINAW

RAILROAD,

IN DIRECT CONNECTION WITH THE

JACKSON, LANSING & SAGINAW,

AND

FORT WAYNE, MUNCIE AND CINCINNATI RAILROADS,

FORMING THE

GREAT SAGINAW ROUTE,

FROM

THE SAGINAW VALLEY

TO

INDIANAPOLIS, ST. LOUIS, LOUISVILLE,

AND ALL SOUTHERN POINTS.

W. A. ERNST, Superintendent.

ROBERT RILLIE, Gen'l Ticket Ag't Ft. W. & L. R. R., Fort Wayne.

JACKSON, LANSING & SAGINAW R. R.

THE MOST DIRECT ROUTE

TO AND FROM

THE SAGINAW VALLEY

AND THE INTERIOR OF

MICHIGAN, OHIO & INDIANA.

IN CONNECTION WITH THE

Fort Wayne, Jackson and Saginaw Railroad

MAKES THE

QUICKEST AND BEST ROUTE

FOR

**Fort Wayne, Muncie, Cincinnati, Logansport, Lafay-
ette, Indianapolis, St. Louis, Louisville,
and all Points in the South.**

TWO THROUGH EXPRESS TRAINS Each Way DAILY

PASSING THROUGH

MASON, LANSING, OWASSO, SAGINAW CITY, EAST SAGINAW,

TO WENONA AND BAY CITY,

CONNECTING AT BAY CITY

WITH STEAMERS TO MACKINAW AND GODRICH.

M. NORTHUP,   A. WATSON,
   Gen'l Freight Ag't, Jackson, Mich.   Superintendent.

THE

ATLANTIC & PACIFIC RAILROAD

Is now open, and running Trains regularly to Seneca, on the
Missouri and Indian Territory Line,

330 Miles Southwest of St. Louis!

This Line, in connection with the "El Paso Mail Line" of new Concord Coaches, forms a

QUICK, CHEAP AND RELIABLE ROUTE

TO ALL POINTS IN

South-West Missouri, South-Eastern Kansas, Northern
Arkansas, Texas and the Indian Territory.

The Atlantic and Pacific Railroad runs through THE GARDEN OF THE UNITED
STATES. The Lands of the Company, consisting of

OVER ONE MILLION OF ACRES,

in Missouri, are now thrown open for settlement, and special inducements are offered
to Emigrants desiring homes in the healthiest portion of the whole country. No long
winters and chilling frosts. The soil is rich and of every variety. Immense deposits
of Zinc, Lead and Iron are found all along the Line.

WE RUN

TWO THROUGH EXPRESS TRAINS DAILY

This is DECIDEDLY THE BEST Route for Freight for all points in Northern Arkansas, Texas and the Indian Territory.
For points on the Upper Arkansas and Red Rivers, shippers can now secure Low Rates
and Prompt Dispatch.

SHIP VIA "ATLANTIC & PACIFIC RAILROAD," AND SAVE INSURANCE.

FOR PARTICULAR INFORMATION,

Apply in person or by letter to E. A. FORD, General Passenger Agent, St. Louis, or

W. H. PATRIARCHE, Gen'l Fr't Ag't,

A. & P. R. R., St. Louis, Mo.

THE MISSOURI PACIFIC RAILROAD

IS THE MOST DIRECT ROUTE TO ALL PARTS OF

WESTERN AND CENTRAL MISSOURI, KANSAS, NEBRASKA,

AND POINTS IN THE GREAT WEST

From its depot, corner Seventh and Poplar streets, St. Louis, the most noted and convenient in the city, it runs through the finest portions of Missouri, in the fertile valleys of the Meramec and Missouri Rivers—a rich and charming country—again striking the Missouri River at Kansas City, there connecting with all lines, North, West and South.

CONNECTIONS ARE CLOSE AND DIRECT FOR

LAWRENCE,	TOPEKA, DENVER,
JUNCTION CITY,	SACRAMENTO,
SALT LAKE CITY.	ST. JOSEPH,
SAN FRANCISCO,	OMAHA,
COUNCIL BLUFFS,	FORT SCOTT,

And all Points in Kansas, Nebraska, Colorado, New Mexico & California.

Frequent and Fast Trains, Smooth Track, Comfortable Sleeping Car Arrangements and Beautiful Scenery, have made this Line a Favorite with the Traveling Public.

☞Through tickets for sale throughout the North, East, and South, and at Company's Offices at 115 North Fourth Street, and Depot, corner Seventh and Poplar streets, St. Louis.

E. A. FORD,   A. A. TALMAGE,
Gen'l Pass'r Ag't, St. Louis.   Gen'l Sup't, St. Louis.

ONLY ALL RAIL LINE SOUTH.

LOUISVILLE & INDIANAPOLIS

RAILROAD.

Three Daily Trains Connecting Direct with

LOUISVILLE & NASHVILLE

AND

MEMPHIS & LOUISVILLE RAILROADS.

FOR

PRINCIPAL SOUTHERN CITIES.

Passengers by this Line Pass over the

GREAT IRON RAILWAY BRIDGE,

.THUS AVOIDING ALL TRANSFERS, FERRIES AND DELAYS.

Purchase Tickets South via Louisville.

CHAS. P. ATMORE,
Gen'l Pass. Agent.

HORACE SCOTT,
Gen'l Supt.

LOUISVILLE AND NASHVILLE

AND

MEMPHIS AND LOUISVILLE

RAILROAD LINE.

SIX DAILY TRAINS

RUNNING FROM

Louisville to Nashville, Memphis and Mobile!

DIRECT CONNECTIONS

WITH

RAILWAYS DIVERGING FROM LOUISVILLE

AND WITH

Louisville and Cincinnati United States Steamers.

With BARDSTOWN BRANCH.
With STAGES FOR MAMMOTH CAVE.
With MEMPHIS AND LOUISVILLE RAILWAY.
With EDGEFIELD AND KENTUCKY RAILWAY.
With RAILWAYS DIVERGING FROM NASHVILLE.
With NASHVILLE AND NORTHWESTERN RAILWAY.
With MOBILE AND OHIO RAILWAY.
With MISSISSIPPI AND TENNESSEE RAILWAY.

ALBERT FINK,
    Gen'l Superintendent.

W. H. KING,
    Gen'l Pass. and Ticket Agent,
        LOUISVILLE.

LOUISVILLE AND CINCINNATI SHORT LINE RAILROAD.

FOUR DAILY TRAINS

BETWEEN

LOUISVILLE & CINCINNATI,

MAKING

DIRECT CONNECTION AT CINCINNATI
WITH TRAINS TO ALL EASTERN POINTS.

AT LOUISVILLE WITH THE

LOUISVILLE, NASHVILLE & MEMPHIS RAILROAD,

FOR ALL POINTS SOUTH.

Round Tickets to Cincinnati and Covington at Reduced Rates.

☞No charge for telegrams to secure sleeping cars.

SAM'L GILL, Sup't.   T. B. JONES, Gen'l Pass. Ag't.

MARIETTA & CINCINNATI RAILROAD

MAKING DIRECT CONNECTIONS WITH

Parkersburg Branch, Baltimore and Ohio Railway, Columbus and
Hocking Valley Railway, Junction of Portsmouth Branch,
Hillsboro' Branch Diverges, and with

RAILWAYS FROM CINCINNATI,

AND WITH

U. S. MAIL STEAMERS.

R. M. FRAYER,   JOHN W. PILLSBURY,
  Gen'l Freight Ag't,   Gen'l Pass. Ag't, Cincinnati, O.